CAMBRIDGE LIBRARY COLLECTION

Books of enduring scholarly value

Women's Writing

The later twentieth century saw a huge wave of academic interest in women's writing, which led to the rediscovery of neglected works from a wide range of genres, periods and languages. Many books that were immensely popular and influential in their own day are now studied again, both for their own sake and for what they reveal about the social, political and cultural conditions of their time. A pioneering resource in this area is Orlando: Women's Writing in the British Isles from the Beginnings to the Present (http://orlando.cambridge.org), which provides entries on authors' lives and writing careers, contextual material, timelines, sets of internal links, and bibliographies. Its editors have made a major contribution to the selection of the works reissued in this series within the Cambridge Library Collection, which focuses on non-fiction publications by women on a wide range of subjects from astronomy to biography, music to political economy, and education to prison reform.

The Women's Victory – and After

Millicent Garrett Fawcett (1847–1929) was an influential writer on political and social matters, especially on topics such as female suffrage and women's education. She was one of the supporters of Newnham College, Cambridge, and was later offered the post of Mistress of Girton, but refused because of her commitment to women's suffrage. She was active as a Suffragist, and opposed the violence of the Suffragette movement. In 1918, women over thirty were given the vote, but this did not end Fawcett's struggle for equal rights, and full suffrage was not achieved until 1928. This work, published in 1920, looks back at the long campaign for women's suffrage, and concludes with an examination of what had actually been achieved in 1918. It supplements her 1911 work *Women's Suffrage, a Short History of the Great Movement*. For more information on this author, see: http://orlando.cambridge.org/public/svPeople?person_id=fawcmi

T0382635

Cambridge University Press has long been a pioneer in the reissuing of out-of-print titles from its own backlist, producing digital reprints of books that are still sought after by scholars and students but could not be reprinted economically using traditional technology. The Cambridge Library Collection extends this activity to a wider range of books which are still of importance to researchers and professionals, either for the source material they contain, or as landmarks in the history of their academic discipline.

Drawing from the world-renowned collections in the Cambridge University Library and other partner libraries, and guided by the advice of experts in each subject area, Cambridge University Press is using state-of-the-art scanning machines in its own Printing House to capture the content of each book selected for inclusion. The files are processed to give a consistently clear, crisp image, and the books finished to the high quality standard for which the Press is recognised around the world. The latest print-on-demand technology ensures that the books will remain available indefinitely, and that orders for single or multiple copies can quickly be supplied.

The Cambridge Library Collection brings back to life books of enduring scholarly value (including out-of-copyright works originally issued by other publishers) across a wide range of disciplines in the humanities and social sciences and in science and technology.

The Women's Victory – and After

Personal Reminiscences, 1911–1918

M ILLICENT G ARRETT F AWCETT

CAMBRIDGE UNIVERSITY PRESS

Cambridge, New York, Melbourne, Madrid, Cape Town,
Singapore, São Paolo, Delhi, Mexico City

Published in the United States of America by Cambridge University Press, New York

www.cambridge.org
Information on this title: www.cambridge.org/9781108026604

© in this compilation Cambridge University Press 2013

This edition first published 1920
This digitally printed version 2013

ISBN 978-1-108-02660-4 Paperback

THE WOMEN'S VICTORY—
AND AFTER

" When there is a fervent aspiration
after better things, springing from a
strong feeling of human brotherhood
and a firm belief in the goodness and
righteousness of God, such aspiration
carries with it an invincible confidence that somehow, somewhere,
somewhen, it must receive its complete fulfilment ; for it is prompted
by the Spirit which fills and orders
the Universe throughout its whole
development."

J. B. MAYOR : *Virgil's Messianic
Eclogue.*

"AT LAST!"

(Reproduced by special permission of the Proprietors of *Punch*.)

Punch, January 23, 1918.]

[*Frontispiece*.

The Women's Victory —and After : Personal Reminiscences, 1911–1918

By Millicent Garrett Fawcett,
LL.D., once President, N.U.W.S.S.

London : Sidgwick & Jackson, Ltd.

First published in 1920

DEDICATORY PREFACE

TO THOSE WHO MADE THE DREAM COME TRUE

I WISH to dedicate this little book to the thousands of faithful friends and gallant comrades whose brave unwearied work, steadfastly maintained through many years, made Women's Suffrage in Great Britain no longer a dream but a reality. Many of them have passed away, but their work, its results, and our gratitude remain. Whether in the flesh or out of the flesh, I have been accustomed to think of them as the Goodly Fellowship of the Prophets: for they foresaw what was coming, proclaimed it, and devoted themselves in making it come in the right way. All my gratitude goes out to them, especially to—

E.G.A. : C.C.O. : E.F.R. : I.O.F. :
A.G. : R.G. : E.P. : E.A. :
R.S. : E.G. : H.A. :
S.G. : I.H.W.:
E.I.

Through the kindness of the Proprietors of *Punch*, I am allowed to use as illustrations some of their excellent pictures demonstrating the growth of the suffrage movement. For this permission, and also for their valued support and sympathy, continued over many years, my heartfelt thanks are hereby tendered.

MILLICENT GARRETT FAWCETT.

LONDON,
January, 1920.

v

CONTENTS

LIST OF ILLUSTRATIONS

(Reproduced by special permission of the Proprietors of "Punch.")

THE WOMEN'S VICTORY—
AND AFTER

CHAPTER I

THE TWO DEPUTATIONS

" I have a passionate love for common justice and common sense."—SYDNEY SMITH.

IN 1911 I wrote a little book called " Women's Suffrage: a Short History of a Great Movement." My intention in the following pages is to bring my story up to February 6th, 1918, when the Royal Assent was given to the Representation of the People Act, which for the first time placed women on the register of parliamentary voters.

In 1911 I ended my book on a note of confidence. I felt quite sure that we were going to win soon, but I did not the least foresee the wonderful series of events which actually led to so complete and great a victory.

Not that all the signs were favourable in 1911— very far from it. There were many ominous clouds on the horizon, and one of the chief of them was the known hostility of Mr. Asquith, then Prime Minister, and at the zenith of his power. His acuteness and dexterity in offence and defence were unrivalled, and most suffragists believed that he intended to wreck our cause on the rocks of Adult Suffrage, for which there had been no demand in the country.

In 1908, almost immediately after he became Prime Minister, Mr. Asquith had announced his intention before the expiration of that Parliament to bring in an Electoral Reform Bill; this Bill, he had declared, would not include women; but he pledged his Government not officially to oppose a woman suffrage amendment "if drafted on democratic lines." The Parliament elected in 1906 with an overwhelming Liberal majority was dissolved in 1909 without the fulfilment of this intention. There were two General Elections in 1910 without the introduction of a Reform Bill. But the suffrage societies continued without intermission to keep up a tremendously active agitation for the enfranchisement of women. The various methods employed have been sufficiently described in my earlier book. It is enough here to state that a large majority of Members of the House of Commons, belonging to all parties, were pledged to support women's suffrage; that various private Members' Bills for extending the franchise to women had passed their second reading in the Commons every year since Mr. Asquith became Prime Minister; that the strength of our support in the rank and file of the Liberal—and also in the Conservative— Party was constantly growing, and that the Labour Party had definitely placed the enfranchisement of women upon its official programme. In January, 1913, immediately after what will be hereafter described as the Franchise Bill fiasco of Mr. Asquith's Government, the Labour Party, at its annual conference, passed by an enormous majority a resolution reaffirming its support of women's suffrage, and calling " upon the party in Parliament to oppose any Franchise Bill in which women are not included." This was the most signal service to our cause which had then been rendered by any political party.

It was followed at the next meeting of the Trades Union Congress by the adoption of the following resolution:

> "That this meeting expresses its deep dissatisfaction with the Government's treatment of the franchise question . . . and protests against the Prime Minister's failure to redeem his repeated pledges to women, and calls upon the Parliamentary Committee to press for the immediate enactment of a Government Reform Bill, which must include the enfranchisement of women."

Over forty trade unions, including the most important, such as the N.U.R. and the A.S.E., adopted resolutions supporting the enfranchisement of women.

The formation of the Conciliation Committee in the House of Commons in 1910 has been sufficiently described in my earlier book (p. 73). Its object was to unite all suffragists in the House, and secure their support for a suffrage Bill which was believed to represent their greatest common measure. They decided that this would be found in a Bill to enfranchise women householders—those women, in fact, who had for about forty years been admitted to the local franchises. The Bill was called the Conciliation Bill because it had reconciled differences existing between various types of suffragists inside the House of Commons.

In July, 1910, two days of the Government's time had been given for a full-dress debate upon the Conciliation Bill. Hostile speeches from Mr. Asquith and Mr. Austen Chamberlain, on the ground of their complete opposition to all kinds of women's suffrage, were followed by equally vehement and hostile speeches from Mr. Lloyd George and Mr. Winston Churchill, on the ground that this particular Bill did not go far enough, and was so drafted as not to admit of amendment. In anticipation of, and during, the Parliamentary debate, *The Times* came out with a hostile article every day for nearly a fortnight, and its columns contained numerous letters prophesying all kinds of horrors and disasters which were to be expected if women were allowed to vote; many were of the type satirized in " Rejected

Addresses," "What fills the Butchers' Shops with Large Blue Flies?" Notwithstanding all this, the division on the Second Reading resulted in a majority of 110 for the Bill, a far larger figure than the Government had been able to command for any of its party measures.

On November 12th, in anticipation of the second General Election in 1910, Mr. Asquith gave a pledge in the House of Commons that his Government would, if still in power, give facilities in the next Parliament for "*proceeding effectively*" with a Bill to enfranchise women if so framed as to permit of free amendment. The second General Election of 1910 took place immediately after this, in December, and again resulted in a majority for Mr. Asquith and the Liberal Party.

On the reassembling of the new House the Conciliation Bill Committee was reformed, Lord Lytton and Mr. Brailsford again acting respectively as chairman and hon. secretary. The Bill was re-drafted on the same lines as regards its provisions, but in a form which admitted of free amendment Our friends were lucky in the ballot, and the debate and division taking place on May 5th, 1911, it was found that the majority of 110 in 1910 had grown to a majority of 167 in 1911—only 88 Members voting against it.

Militantism, or, as it would now be called, "direct action," had been suspended from the beginning of 1911 in view of Mr. Asquith's promise to grant time for " proceeding effectively " with all the stages of a Suffrage Bill during that Session. It should be noted that these two suffrage victories in the House of Commons in July, 1910, and May, 1911, had taken place, in each case, when Members were fresh from contact with their constituencies after the General Elections of January and December, 1910. The contrary was often most ignorantly, if not maliciously, asserted by antisuffragists. After the big majority for the Conciliation Bill in May, 1911, Mr. Lloyd George promised that in the next Session a week of Government time should be given for the Second Reading and further stages of the Bill, assuming, of course, its having received a Second Reading. Sir Edward Grey further explained the value of this offer, and said (June 1st, 1911) that a definite opportunity had been promised to the House of Commons, and that it was important that people should understand that it was a " real opportunity," and " not a bogus offer." In a letter to Lord Lytton, dated June 15th, Mr. Asquith endorsed what Sir Edward Grey (now Viscount Grey of Fallodon) had said; and writing again on August 23rd, he made it clear that his promise applied to the Conciliation Bill, and not to any other women's suffrage measure. Therefore it was not astonishing that suffragists of all shades of opinion had high hopes of a real victory in the Session of 1912.

Then came, quite suddenly, a characteristic blow from Mr. Asquith. On November 7th, 1911, in answer to a deputation of the People's Suffrage Federation, introduced by Mr. Arthur Henderson, M.P., Mr Asquith stated that he intended to introduce an Electoral Reform Bill during the coming Session of 1912. This Bill was to be on very wide lines; all existing franchises were to be swept away, plural voting abolished, and the period of residence materially reduced. The vote in this Bill was, Mr. Asquith said, to be based on male citizenship. His exact words were: " We believe a man's right to vote depends on his being a citizen, and *primâ facie* a man who is a citizen *of full age and competent understanding* ought to be entitled to a vote." When pressed by Mr. Henderson to say what he intended to do about women, he dismissed the inquiry with the curt remark that his opinions on the subject were well known, and had suffered no modification or change during the last few years.

The announcement made a tremendous stir, and not in suffrage circles only. The women's point of view was strongly urged in many quarters, and to an unprecedented extent by a large proportion of the general Press throughout the country.

Our own paper, *The Common Cause*, pointed out the bad statesmanship which acknowledged " the intolerable slur of disfranchisement " where men were concerned, and professed a desire to extend the franchise to all citizens of full age and competent understanding, and yet did nothing to remove this intolerable slur from the women of the country, and thus by implication accepted the theory that women should be held in the bondage of perpetual nonage, and could never be rightly described as of competent understanding.

If this attitude on Mr. Asquith's part was intended to provoke a renewed outburst of militantism, it certainly had the desired effect. Even the mildest and most pacific of suffragists felt that she had received from the Prime Minister a personal insult. One of them, by no means identified up to that time with militant tactics, wrote to the Press that Mr. Asquith's words " had filled her with an impulse of blind rage." Those who represented the constitutional suffrage movement constantly felt themselves in face of a double danger—the discredit to their movement of the window smashing and other unjustifiable methods of violence, and the continued and often very subtle opposition of the head of the party most identified with the advocacy of parliamentary reform.

The joint deputation of all the suffrage societies to Mr. Asquith on November 18th, 1911, has been sufficiently described in what I call my first volume. I may, however, here be allowed to repeat that, on behalf of the National Union of

Women's Suffrage Societies, four categorical questions were then put to Mr. Asquith:

1. Was it the intention of the Government that the Reform Bill should be passed through all its stages in the Session of 1912?

2. Will the Bill be drafted in such a manner as to admit of amendments introducing women on other terms than men?

3. Will the Government undertake not to oppose such amendments?

4. Will the Government regard any amendment enfranchising women which is carried in the House of Commons as an integral part of the Bill, to be defended by the Government in all its later stages?

To each of these questions Mr. Asquith gave the answer, absolutely unqualified and unconditioned, " Certainly."

His whole attitude and manner were far more conciliatory than they had ever been before, and, whether designedly or not, certainly had the effect of strengthening our hopes of a speedy victory. Referring to his own position, he said: " It is perfectly consistent with the self-respect and the best traditions of our public life that in relation to a question which divides parties, not only the head of the Government, but the Government itself, should say that if the House of Commons on its responsibility is prepared to transform or extend a measure which we are agreed in thinking necessary

—a measure for the franchise as regards men—and to confer the franchise on women, we shall not only acquiesce in that proposal, but we shall treat it as the considered judgment of Parliament, and shall make ourselves responsible for carrying it out."

What a contrast these suave words presented to Mr. Asquith's method of receiving earlier suffrage deputations only those who had taken part in both could fully appreciate.

Mr. Lloyd George was present, and was pressed by the deputation to speak. He did so very briefly, and said: " I shall take the first opportunity of setting forth my views in reference to this matter. . . . The only thing I would say now is this, and I say it after twenty-one years' experience of Parliament: Do not commit yourselves too readily to the statement that this is a trick upon women's suffrage. If you find next year as a result of this ' trick ' that several millions of women have been added in a Bill to the franchise, that this Bill has been sent to the House of Lords by the Government, and that the Government stand by that Bill, whatever the Lords do,* then those who have committed themselves to that ill-conditioned suggestion will look very foolish."

That closed the deputation; but Mr. Lloyd George sent the following message to the National Union

* This pointed to the probable application of the Parliament Act to the proposed Reform Bill.

almost immediately afterwards: "The Prime Minister's pronouncement as to the attitude to be adopted by the Government towards the question seems to me to make the carrying of a women's suffrage amendment on broad democratic lines to next year's Franchise Bill a certainty. I am willing to do all in my power to help those who are labouring to reach a successful issue in the coming Session. Next year provides the supreme opportunity, and nothing but unwise handling of that chance can compass failure."

No doubt Mr. Lloyd George's reference to the risk of unwise handling was directed to the suffragists themselves. But it was soon to be proved that "unwise handling" was quite as likely to proceed from the head of the Government. Mr. Asquith had received the suffragists on November 18th. Twenty-six days after this, on December 14th, he received an antisuffrage deputation. It was introduced by Lord Curzon, and among those who spoke were Mrs. Humphry Ward, Miss Violet Markham, and Sir C. Henry. Mr. MacCallum Scott, Member for Bridgeton, Glasgow, was also present. In the course of his reply, Mr. Asquith made it quite clear that his sympathies were entirely with the deputation; and he encouraged them to put more vigour into their methods of opposing the extension of the franchise to women, advising them "to take off their coats," or whatever was "the equivalent raiment to which he should allude when addressing ladies."

He also chaffed them genially about the Referendum, a subject on which the deputation had not been able to agree among themselves. All this was quite good sword-play, and no reasonable suffragists could fairly object to it. But there was one passage in his reply to which they did most vehemently object, as they felt that it went far to render perfectly worthless the reassuring words he had addressed to themselves about three weeks earlier. The words to which we objected were these: " As an individual I am in entire agreement with you that the grant of the parliamentary suffrage to women in this country *would be a political mistake of a very disastrous kind.*" How could a Prime Minister reconcile it with his responsibility to his country to acquiesce in and help to carry through all its stages in both Houses of Parliament a constitutional change which he himself believed to be " a political mistake of a very disastrous kind " ?

One member of the antisuffrage deputation, Mr. MacCallum Scott, M.P., interpreted this expression of his political chief as an S.O.S. call to his party, and in a letter addressed to the *Standard* early in the following Session he called upon his brother Liberal M.P.'s, whether they were pledged to suffrage or not, to rally to the support of the Prime Minister and to deliver him from " the humiliation " of having to fulfil the promises he had made to the suffragists recounted in the earlier pages of this chapter.

From this time every possible intrigue and trick and misrepresentation were resorted to in order to defeat the suffragists when they next submitted their question to the vote of the House of Commons. Nevertheless, our strongest friends inside the Government continued to be very confident. In December, Sir Edward Grey, Mr. Asquith's Foreign Secretary, and a very leading member of the Government, and Mr. Lloyd George, then Chancellor of the Exchequer, addressed a large meeting of the Women's Liberal Federation in the Horticultural Hall, Westminster. Sir Edward Grey spoke strongly and very reassuringly about the practical certainty of the addition of women's suffrage to the coming Government Reform Bill, and Mr. Lloyd George made an eloquent speech in the same sense. The event proved them to have been entirely mistaken, not through our blundering, but in consequence of serious mistakes made by the Government itself.

Looking back over the last years of our struggle, we could not but see that our chief antagonist was Mr. Asquith. Opposition from a Liberal, with all the Liberal traditions of devotion to the principles of representative government and a wide suffrage, was far more damaging to our cause than opposition from Conservatives. It was Mr. Asquith, more

than any other one person, who prevented the
Liberal Party becoming a Reform Party, and
including women in their general scheme of enfranchisement. In 1906, very shortly after the
unprecedented Liberal triumph of that year, the
Liberals returned were by an immense majority
supporters of the enfranchisement of women. Sir
Henry Campbell-Bannerman, the Prime Minister,
was one of these, and received a large representative
suffrage deputation in May of that year. He told
them that they had made out a " conclusive and
irrefutable case," but promised them no practical
action whatever from the Government of which
he was the head; the only advice which he gave
the deputation was that they should go on " pester-
ing." He evidently thought that the best course
for suffragists to pursue was to make themselves
as great a nuisance as possible until their claim
was granted. There must have been obstacles in
his own Government which prevented his giving
us any more favourable answer, and there can be
little doubt that these obstacles were not so much
to be found among the Harcourts and the Hobhouses,
but in the more formidable personality of his Home
Secretary, Mr. Asquith, who was destined, as events
proved, within less than two years to be his successor
as Prime Minister. Mr. Asquith had no grasp
whatever of the significance of our movement.
When what was called " militancy " came upon the

scene, very much encouraged, of course, by Sir H. Campbell-Bannerman's speech, he did not attribute it, as he should have done, to the consequences of justice long delayed; he saw nothing in it but a means of defeating the whole movement, opportunities for covering its supporters with ridicule and himself with additional prestige. Thus he would in a public speech compare himself with Orpheus, and the whole suffrage party—for he then made no distinction between militants and non-militants—with the wild women of Thrace. We were " the rout that made the hideous war," and he, with mock humility, our victim. He never really understood the social and educational changes in the position of women which had been going on for the last two generations, and made a corresponding change in their political status an urgent necessity. One of his chief weapons against us was this assumed inability to distinguish between the militants and non-militants, and this was quite as much marked in the early stages of the militant movement, when nothing more tragic had been done than asking inconvenient questions at meetings, waving flags, and making speeches in the lobby of the House, and so forth, as it was later, when the militant movement became month by month increasingly aggressive and dangerous. A statesman, whether in England, India, Ireland, or Egypt, face to face with grave and persistent disorder, while taking immediate steps to restore order, does not content himself with the mere employment of physical force; he enquires into the moral causes of the disorder, and seeks by wise legislation to remove them. This Mr. Asquith never did in regard to women; for his eleventh hour conversion to women's suffrage, although welcome, was more then for his own good than ours. *Punch's* picture of the " Conductorette " helping Mr. Asquith into the suffrage bus, with the exclamation, " Come along, sir; better late than never," exactly described his position in 1917.

I well remember the long series of suffrage deputations which it fell to my lot to introduce to Mr. Asquith, and his gradual change of manner in receiving us. Some of the incidents of these interviews were extremely amusing, and we laughed over them as soon as we were by ourselves. The first was when he was Chancellor of the Exchequer in Sir Henry Campbell-Bannerman's Government. We had with us Miss Emily Davies, the founder of Girton College; Lady Strachey, wife of the well-known Indian administrator; Miss Frances Sterling; Miss I. O. Ford; and other well-known suffrage leaders from our various societies. While we were still in the waiting-room, I was sent for by myself for a preliminary interview with Mr. Asquith's private secretary. I found him a rather agitated-looking young man, who said: " I want you, Mrs. Fawcett,

THE CATCH OF THE SEASON.

Conductorette (to Mr. Asquith) : " Come along, sir ; better late than never."

(Reproduced by special permission of the Proprietors of *Punch*.)

Punch, April 4, 1917.]

[Facing page 16.

to give me your personal word of honour that no member of your deputation will employ physical violence." " Indeed," I replied, " you astonish me. I had no idea you were so frightened." He instantly repudiated being frightened, and I rejoined: " Someone must be frightened, or such a request would never have been made of me; but as it is made, without hesitation I give you my most solemn word of honour that no member of my deputation will either employ or threaten violence." The idea of it, considering who they were, entertained me, and I took no pains to conceal my amusement. I rejoined my deputation, and almost instantly the gentleman I had just left reappeared to conduct us to the reception room, I walking first, side by side with the secretary. As we entered the room, where Mr. Asquith was sitting with his back to the light on our right, I observed in the opposite corner on our extreme left a lady I did not know. So I said to the secretary in a clear voice, " I give no guarantee for that lady; I do not know her." "Oh, that," he rejoined, and again showed some agitation— " that lady is Miss Asquith." Members of the deputation told me afterwards that they had also seen Mrs. Asquith sitting behind her husband's chair, but I did not see her myself.* I remember

* In view of the promise which had just been exacted of me not to use violence towards the Chancellor, the

2

the extremely forbidding expression of Mr. Asquith's face, and how, after a little, when I was speaking to him, I ceased to look at him on this account, and looked at the space just above his head. Of course he gave us no encouragement. One of his expressions was that he "had yet to learn that there was any widely spread desire among women themselves for their enfranchisement." A member of the deputation, Miss I. O. Ford, of Leeds, who all her life had been very much in sympathy and in constant communication with industrial women in the North of England, replied to this, that if Mr. Asquith would come with her to meetings of working-women in Yorkshire, she could show him that there were thousands of women who keenly desired the vote. He replied, in his most forbidding air: "The prospect does not greatly attract me."

This interview was a specimen of Mr. Asquith in his most hostile mood. It was our lot to taste the insolence of office and the proud man's contumely. It was part of our job. We rather resented being made a show of for the benefit of his family; but this, after all, was a small matter. His manner, possibly

___

presence of his wife and daughter might have been explained on the hypothesis that in the event of assault and battery on our part they could have flung their persons between their husband and father and his assailants. But this possible explanation of the presence of these ladies did not occur to me at the time.

adopted to impress his wife and daughter, was indicative of his deeply seated opposition to our aims, and it was extremely interesting to watch how, by slow degrees, it was modified until it became, even while he was still in opposition to us, cordial and pleasant. Once, I remember, I could not resist saying to him that I had never seen a man so much improved. But this was very near the time when our victory was a certainty.

CHAPTER II

THE DEFEAT OF THE CONCILIATION BILL

" Keep on ploughing when you've missed crops,
Keep on dancing when the fiddle stops,
Keep on faithful till the curtain drops,
And you'll get there in the morning."
    (*With acknowledgments to the Trent Otter.*)

SUFFRAGISTS had entered upon the Session of 1912 with two strings to their bow. The first was a definite promise from the Prime Minister of a week, or more if necessary, of parliamentary time for the Second Reading and all the necessary subsequent stages of the Conciliation Bill.

The second string was embodied in the series of promises given by Mr. Asquith to the suffrage deputation described in the last chapter. These promises we had been assured by Mr. Lloyd George were of the very utmost value; to cast doubt upon them was " an imputation of deep dishonour " which he vehemently repudiated. Sir Edward Grey shared Mr. Lloyd George's opinion, and assured us that we now had " a real opportunity " of victory.

Our first struggle was over the Second Reading

of the Conciliation Bill, and it was not long before
we discovered that the dice were being loaded
against us.   We had, however, in our favour the
big majorities for the Bill in 1910 and 1911, the
promises and past support of M.P.'s of all the parties,
numbering more than half the House of Commons.
This position seemed too strong to be abandoned,
and we therefore encouraged our friends in the
House to ballot for a day for the Second Reading.
The 28th of March was secured.   The text and title
of the Bill were exactly the same as had been read
a second time the previous year by a majority of
167.

As the day for the Second Reading approached we
became aware that all kinds of new influences
hostile to us were in operation.   These were for the
most part in the nature of Lobby gossip, and, not
being publicly made, could not be publicly refuted.
One, however, had been made public—viz., Mr. Mac-
Callum Scott's appeal to Liberals, published in the
Standard, as mentioned in the last chapter, not to
allow their leader, Mr. Asquith, to be subjected to
" the humiliation " of having to fulfil the promises
he had given to suffragists in the previous November.
This method of detaching Liberal M.P.'s from the
support of the Bill was very freely used.   It was
said that if this Bill were carried it would break up
the Ministry, and in particular it was widely
rumoured that the Prime Minister and other anti-

suffrage members of the Government would resign. These rumours were never contradicted. Mr. Lloyd George's name was also freely used in this connection. Had he not openly expressed his dislike of the Bill ? He had spoken against it in 1910; and in his speech at Bath in November, 1911, he had boasted that it had been " torpedoed " by the promise of a wider measure. The Irish Nationalists were peculiarly susceptible to the line of argument that the success of women's suffrage would mean the break up of the Government. The Home Rule Bill had been passed in all its stages twice by the House of Commons in two successive Sessions, but it required, under the Parliament Act, to be passed three times in three successive Sessions before it could be placed on the Statute Book, notwithstanding its rejection by the House of Lords. The continued violence of the militants—smashing windows, slashing the canvas of valuable pictures, burning the contents of letter-boxes, letting off explosives in empty churches, etc.—caused intense irritation and re-sentment among the general public, and afforded an excuse to those M.P.'s who had promised their support to our movement to break their word. On March 28th thirteen members of the Labour Party were absent in their constituencies in conse-quence of the labour unrest connected with the coal strike. The result of this combination of unfavour-able conditions resulted in the defeat of the Bill by a majority of 14. Our Labour supporters could have saved the Bill had they been present in their full strength. It was a heavy disappointment, and the utmost was of course made of it by the anti-suffragists, including, first and foremost, Mr. Asquith.

Analyzing the causes of our defeat, we found that, whereas in 1911 thirty-one followers of Mr. John Redmond had supported the Bill, including Mr. William Redmond, Professor Kettle, Mr. Stephen Gwynn, and other men in a leading position in their party, in 1912 not a single one voted for it. The only Irish Nationalists who continued their support to the Bill were three O'Brienites, Mr. William O'Brien himself, Mr. Timothy Healy, and Mr. Gilhooley. Twenty-two Liberals, twelve Nationalists, and eight Conservatives, who had hitherto supported the Bill, now voted against it. A far larger number withdrew their support, but did not give a hostile vote.

What perturbed us more than anything else was the knowledge that the same underhand and unscrupulous methods which had been used to defeat the Conciliation Bill would also in all probability be used to defeat the women's suffrage amendments to the Government Reform Bill. We appealed, quite unsuccessfully, to our leading friends in the Government to check these hostile influences.

One outstanding instance of the methods employed

against us must here be described. Some years
before, Dr. Louisa Martindale, a lady of the highest
character and professional standing, belonging to
a family universally respected in their place of
residence in the South of England, had written a book
called " Beneath the Surface." It was, in a far briefer
form, on the lines of Mr. A. Flexner's well-known
book on the History of Prostitution in Europe.
It was in part historical and in part a warning to men
and women of the physical risks connected with
promiscuous sexual intercourse, and its dangers
to the race as well as to the individual. The
literature department of the N.U.W.S.S. stocked
this volume, and placed its title in the list of books
and pamphlets they were prepared to supply. Then
suddenly there appeared in the list of questions
to be addressed by M.P.'s to members of the
Government one by the Marquis of Tullibardine
(now the Duke of Atholl), to ask the Home Secretary
if he intended to prosecute the N.U.W.S.S. for
circulating an " obscene book," meaning the one
by Dr. Martindale. The Home Secretary, Mr. R.
McKenna, could give no positive answer; he must
take time to make enquiries; the question must be
repeated. A few days later it was repeated; again
the Home Secretary delayed his reply; he found it
necessary to consult the Law Officers. The Under
Secretary for the Home Department answered
these questions more than once, but at last owned

that the Law Officers advised that a prosecution would not be successful. As no one in his senses could possibly think that this little book was obscene, it would have been simpler to reply that the prosecution would be unsuccessful on this account; but this straightforward course was avoided. It became evident to us that the object of the whole business was to bring up the question in the House of Commons as often as possible with a view of prejudicing the public against the suffrage and the suffragists, and to produce the impression that we were people who delighted in the circulation of vile literature. This went on for about a fortnight, when I happened to have the opportunity of a conversation, on an entirely different subject, with a highly placed officer of the Government, a member of the House of Lords. While I was talking to him on the subject on which I had come to see him, it occurred to me to speak to him also about the little plot to discredit the suffrage movement in which the Home Secretary was playing the leading rôle. " Is it with your knowledge and consent, Lord ——," I asked, " that your colleague, Mr. McKenna, is keeping before the public as long as he possibly can the interesting fact that he is unable to make up his mind whether or not to prosecute me and the N.U.W.S.S., of which I am President, for circulating obscene literature ? Three questions have already been asked on this subject in the House of Commons

within the last eleven days, and it is impossible
to say how many more times the point will be discussed in the House and reported in every paper in
Great Britain."* I also told him something of
Dr. Louisa Martindale, her high character and
first-rate professional position, and also (rather
maliciously on my part) that her family were very
active and highly esteemed Liberals in Sussex,
and that gratuitous insults to them would be keenly
resented, and might possibly even have a political
reaction. He appeared startled, and, as far as I
could gather, had had no previous knowledge of
what had been going on. He said very little, and
promised me nothing. But from that date the
attack upon Dr. Martindale, her book, and the
N.U.W.S.S., entirely ceased. The incident did not
increase our esteem for the antisuffrage party in the
House of Commons. A few months later I had
proof, if proof were needed, that the Government
did not seriously believe me to be a person capable
of circulating obscene literature, for I was invited
by the Government to become a member of the
Royal Commission on Venereal Disease, a position
which could certainly not have been offered if the
Government had shared Mr. McKenna's doubts

* Antisuffragists in the country had taken up the campaign of calumny against us and had spoken of suffragists
as " purveyors of vile literature," disseminators of " pesti-
lential doctrines," and had used other flowers of rhetoric
of the same description.

as to my character. I was not able to accept the invitation because my suffrage work entirely absorbed me, and I saw no prospect of its claims becoming less urgent in the near future.

The Session of 1912 dragged its interminable length along. It lasted for thirteen months, from January, 1912, to January, 1913, both inclusive. The Government were slow in producing their Reform Bill. In May, however, it was brought forward, and it did not come up for Second Reading until July 12th, 1912. In the Second Reading debate Mr. Asquith, Prime Minister and Leader of the House, expressed himself as follows:

" This Bill does not propose to confer the franchise on women; whatever extensions of the franchise it makes are to male persons only. Speaking for myself, I cannot help remembering that the House at an earlier stage of the Session rejected with, I think, sufficient emphasis the proposal to confer the franchise on women; and, so far as I am concerned, I dismiss at this moment as altogether improbable the hypothesis that the House of Commons is likely to stultify itself by reversing in the same Session the considered judgment at which it has arrived."

That is to say, the rejection of the Conciliation Bill by a majority of 14 in the previous March was to be taken as " the considered judgment of the House of Commons," whereas its passage in May, 1911, by a majority of 167 counted for nothing at all. What the passage just quoted did stand for was the continued and bitter hostility of the Prime Minister to women's suffrage in any form, and as a renewal of his S.O.S. call to his followers to come to his deliverance.   The fortunes of all the little politicians " in the make " are absolutely in the hands of the Prime Minister—more so at that moment than perhaps at any other period of our history.   To please the Prime Minister and serve his purposes indicated the road which led to success and preferment, and he made it absolutely plain what was the best possible way to please him in this matter of women's enfranchisement.

This was truly a time when we had " to go on dancing when the fiddle stopped," and we did not decline the task.   We held two immense meetings in the Albert Hall, the combined collections at which totalled nearly £13,000, and also organized an even more than usually vigorous campaign throughout the country in support of the inclusion of women in the Government Reform Bill: there were twenty-one by-elections during the year, in all of which the N.U.W.S.S. took an active part, making suffrage a very live issue in the country, and we also lost no opportunity of raising the question in the House on other Bills which came before it.

But the change from a majority of 167 in 1911 to a minority of 14 in 1912 gave a fatal shock to what had hitherto been our election policy—namely, the support at all contested elections of the candidate (irrespective of party) whom we deemed from his answers to our questions, his personal record, and other indications, to be " the best friend of women's suffrage." When the Conciliation Bill was defeated in March, 1912, 42 of these " best friends " had voted against the Bill, and 91 had abstained from supporting it. To lean on such " friends " as these was to lean on a broken reed. We did not abandon the essential principle of our election policy, but we gave a new and improved interpretation of the meaning to be attributed to the words " best friend "; and as a result of a special council held for the purpose in May, 1912, it was decided that a friend of suffrage who had the support of his party upon our question was a better friend than one who belonged to a party which was either hostile or neutral. The immense powers of party in our politics made it practically certain that this was the only safe line to take. There were, it is true, a handful of men, in both the Liberal and Conservative ranks, who had shown themselves such strong and convinced suffragists as to be capable of disregarding the party whip when it was used against us. These we defined as " tried friends "—tried not only on the platform, but in the fiery ordeal of the House of Commons, and these we excepted from the new definition we had agreed to make of the words " the best friend of women's suffrage."

CHAPTER III

THE ELECTION FIGHTING FUND

" My centre is giving way, my right wing is falling back. The situation is excellent. I am attacking."— MARSHAL FOCH TO G.H.Q.

THE change of policy indicated at the end of the last chapter was adopted after full deliberation and discussion at a council meeting at which our 411 societies were represented, and at which, as was to be expected, there was an important minority who objected to it. For at this council we resolved on a change of rules. The general objects of the N.U.W.S.S. in by-elections were defined as follows:

1. To shorten the term of office of the Cabinet as at present constituted, especially by opposing antisuffrage Ministers.
2. To strengthen any party in the House of Commons which adopts women's suffrage as part of its official programme.

At by-elections we decided that the N.U. should support those candidates whose return would best promote the foregoing objects, provided that:

(a) No Government candidate should be supported.

(*b*) No candidate shall be supported who does not answer all the National Union questions in the affirmative.

Another clause provided for the exemption of " tried friends " from these regulations. It would, of course, have been an absurdity for suffragists to oppose such men as the late Mr. Walter McLaren or Lord Robert Cecil, who had shown through the stress and strain of many years of parliamentary life that they were prepared to act independently of party in cases where electoral justice to women was involved.

But our change of policy was in effect a declaration of war against the official Liberal Party and of support of the Labour Party, which was the only party which had made women's suffrage part of its programme.

This not unnaturally laid us open to the charge of having abandoned our non-party attitude; but I thought at the time, and I think still, that it was the only possible attitude for a truly non-party association such as ours to adopt. We were making no break with our non-party professions so long as we were prepared to give our whole-hearted support to any party which made the enfranchisement of women part of its programme. We found analogies in the attitude of other non-party organizations, and also in what was happening in the suffrage work in Sweden. In our own country we were

so far fortunate that none of the political parties
had officially identified itself with opposition to
suffrage.   Men of unrivalled distinction in the
Conservative Party for many years past had supported women's suffrage; the names of Lord
Beaconsfield, Lord Salisbury (the great Prime
Minister), Mr. Arthur Balfour, Lord John Manners,
Lord Robert Cecil, need only be mentioned to show
that it was an absolute impossibility for the Conservative Party, as a party, to oppose women's
suffrage.   The same could be said for the Liberals,
past and present: The Hon. Charles Villiers, Mr. J.
S. Mill, Sir H. Campbell-Bannerman, Sir Edward
Grey, Mr. Lloyd George, Mr. Acland, and Sir John
Simon, held the antisuffragists in their own party
in check; moreover, the rank and file of Liberals
were largely in our favour, and all the Liberal catch-
words could be cited *ad nauseam* in our support.
There could therefore be absolutely no question
of opposition to women's franchise becoming an
item in the Liberal programme.

In Sweden, however, the Conservative Party
had definitely identified itself with antisuffragism;
and the Swedish Suffrage Society, non-party like
our own, had been obliged by force of circumstances
to put itself into opposition to the party in their
own country which definitely opposed the one
object for which their society existed.

We no doubt occupied an analogous position

with regard to our own political situation; but we had a very important advantage in the existence of one party, the Labour Party, which had officially accepted women's suffrage, and had shown the sincerity of its support by being willing to record its votes in the House in favour of a limited form of enfranchisement for women, although its own inclinations, and probably also its party interests, were in favour of a much more extended measure. The Swedish suffragists opposed the one party which had made hostility to their enfranchisement part of its programme; the N.U.W.S.S. supported the one party which had taken the opposite course by definitely adopting women's suffrage as part of its programme. I maintain that by so doing neither the Swedish nor the British suffrage societies forfeited their claim to describe themselves as " non-party." We welcomed members of all parties into our ranks, and were prepared to give impartial support to any party which made our object its own.

It is interesting now to look back at the N.U.W.S.S. report in the year 1912, and to see the care with which we defined our position. No Government candidate was to be supported, because the Government, under Mr. Asquith, had shown the most determined opposition to our enfranchisement. When a Conservative candidate was supported, it was because we deemed this the best way of securing

the defeat of a Government candidate; when the
Labour candidate was supported, it was made clear
that this was done because the Labour Party was
the only party which had made women's suffrage
part of its programme, and had, moreover, rendered
us the signal service of calling upon its parliamentary representatives to oppose any Franchise Bill
which did not include women.

A society which disregarded such signal services
as these could only be described as abandoning its
non-party attitude and identifying itself with
opposition to those who had shown themselves the
strongest supporters of our movement.

It was not enough for us to put on record our
intention of doing our best to strengthen the
position of the Labour Party at by-elections; we
also made plans to help Labour members to defend
their seats at the time of a general election. A
special committee was formed to organize the
support of Labour candidates, and to raise a sum
of money for this purpose. It was thus that the
Election Fighting Fund was inaugurated in May,
1912. Two thousand pounds was at once subscribed
in the room, before any special appeal had been
made; and during the short time between the
starting of the fund and the outbreak of the European
War it was sufficiently replenished by constant
gifts from our own members to enable us to keep
up the work with vigour and efficiency. The fund

had not been a month in existence before it was used in support of the Labour candidate at the Holmfirth by-election; and there were shortly afterwards three other by-elections—at Hanley, Crewe, and Midlothian—at which the Election Fighting Fund and its band of organizers and speakers were used in support of Labour candidates. We were authoritatively assured that the Liberals knew that they would have held the seats at Crewe and Midlothian had the attitude of their party been satisfactory on women's suffrage. In 1913 the E.F.F. work was put into operation at Houghton-le-Spring, Keighley, and Lanark; and in 1914 in North-West Durham, Leith Burghs, and North-East Derbyshire. There were therefore ten elections in all during the almost exactly two years in which the E.F.F. policy was vigorously worked by the N.U.W.S.S., and during which six seats, counting for twelve votes in a division, were transferred from the Liberal to the Conservative side of the House. We were very well satisfied by these results, although of course disappointed that no Labour candidate had won a seat: in every case, however, the number of votes recorded for Labour had greatly increased. We had a splendid band of first-class speakers and organizers to work in each constituency; and at each successive election the whole place rang with women's suffrage and our meetings were crowded and enthusiastic—very often

much more crowded and enthusiastic than those of
the candidates. In the first election the Liberal
against whom we had worked got in, but his majority
was reduced to less than half what it had been
at the last contest. The next election was less
satisfactory; but at the third, a seat formerly held
by a Liberal by a majority of 1,704 was gained by
a Conservative supporter of suffrage, and it was
generally acknowledged in the district that the
vigorous help of the N.U.W.S.S. was the deciding
factor in defeating the Liberal candidate. The
Labour candidate polled nearly double the number
of votes which his party had secured at the last
three-cornered contest, and consequently was the
means of securing the defeat of the Government
candidate. Our success at Crewe was followed by a
still more notable victory in Midlothian, the famous
seat won by Mr. Gladstone in 1879, and from
that date looked upon as an impregnable stronghold
of Liberalism. In September, 1912, the former
Liberal majority of 3,157 was converted into a
Conservative majority of 32, the Labour candidate, who stood for the first time, polling 2,413
votes.

It is unnecessary to go in detail through the rest
of the elections in which the N.U. in 1913, and up
to June, 1914, worked the E.F.F. policy for all they
were worth; the specimens of which I have given
details are indicative of the remainder. When

we were originally discussing our change of election policy, Mr. H. N. Brailsford, who had warmly pressed it upon us, said to us, " The moment that you are able by your election work to transfer seats from one side of the House of Commons to the other, the Whips and the wire-pullers will begin to treat you with respect "; and we certainly found that this was the case. In every election in which the E.F.F. committee took part, women's suffrage was the main topic of the contest, and in every case, although we did not succeed in winning the seats for Labour candidates, the value of our work in their behalf was most warmly recognized. We never in any case subsidized the Labour candidates. Their independence was jealously preserved by their own party, and correspondingly respected by us; any attempt to infringe it would have been deeply resented. Our work in the constituency was strictly our own; we held meetings, organized processions and other demonstrations, and paid our own way with the funds our own members had subscribed for the purpose. We had nothing to conceal, nor had the Labour men for whom we worked.

The N.U.W.S.S. had always interpreted " non-party " to mean that the N.U. included members of all parties within its ranks. We therefore naturally chose as our speakers and organizers to carry out.our E.F.F. work from among those of our members whose personal sympathies were with the Labour Party.

The whole movement had been a source of strength to our Union, and we were looking forward to further developments when all schemes for this object were cut short by the outbreak of war on August 4th, 1914. A special meeting of the E.F.F. committee was held immediately, and decided at once that during the war the Election Fighting Fund should be used to employ the E.F.F. staff for the time being on relief work only. This will be further described in a future chapter, which will deal with the general activities of the N.U.W.S.S. during the war.

CHAPTER IV

THE FIASCO OF THE GOVERNMENT REFORM BILL

"If we can't win as fast as we could wish, we know that in the long run our opponents cannot win at all."— JOHN BRIGHT.

WE were at this time receiving a great deal of good advice from suffrage members of the Cabinet. One of them, who ought to have known better, advised us to rouse public opinion in our support. " Why," he said, " do you not hold a few meetings, and get good speakers, like Miss Royden, to address them ?" We replied that we had held 4,000 public meetings in the last four months, filling the largest halls again and again, and that Miss Royden, never very robust, had nearly killed herself by fulfilling the constant demands that were made upon her for speeches at our innumerable demonstrations. She had spoken 267 times in the last twelve months. We reminded him that there had been no agitation at all by men for a wider franchise for themselves; there had been a persistent and strenuous demand by women for their own enfranchisement; and the only official reply of the Government was to promise a Bill for more suffrage to men, and no suffrage at all for women. All this was, of course, so much more grist to the mill at which we had to grind out perpetual speeches. This, as we did not fail to point out, illustrated the value of a vote: voters could get what they wanted without even asking for it; whereas the voteless had to devote years and generations, and to spend thousands of pounds, in order to voice persistent demands on the part of women for representation, demands which were as persistently and determinedly passed by unnoticed, and we were asked why we did not hold a few meetings! The House of Commons seems scarcely capable of giving intelligent attention to any subject unless it is forced to undertake the excruciating pain of thought by the demands made by voters in the constituencies. The most remarkable social revolution had been taking place for the last fifty years in the educational and professional and industrial status of women; all we asked was that a corresponding change should be made in their political status; but up to the present the only reply we could get from the Government had been rightly described by one of its members as " shuffling and delay."

At this time we derived a sort of sorry consolation by the articles which appeared in the Press on the expiration of the twenty years during which the development of motor travelling in this country had been held back by ignorant legislation. The public were reminded that the first Act passed by Parliament in regard to automobile traffic enjoined that motors must not exceed the pace of four miles an hour, and must be preceded by a man on foot waving a red flag! The moral for us was that if our legislators could so little read the signs of the times in regard to a comparatively simple matter like the development of motor transport, it was not astonishing that they were at least as incapable of reading the signs of the times in regard to a great human movement which was gradually, in almost every part of the world, raising the position of women from absolute subjection to free citizenship Our spirits were raised, too, by the fact that, though we were not winning in our own Parliament, we were winning in other Parliaments and everywhere else. A Czech woman had been returned to the Diet in Bohemia; and three new States were won for suffrage in the U.S.A. Barriers in other directions were everywhere breaking down. The very same papers which reported Mr. Asquith's reception of the antisuffrage deputation in December, 1911, when he confessed his unaltered and unalterable opposition to women's suffrage, also contained the announcement of the election of the first woman to the fellowship of the Royal College of Surgeons. The more intelligent of the antisuffragists, such as Mrs. Humphry Ward, were constantly proclaiming their sympathy with every step in the development of women's freedom which had already been won, such as their share in, and responsibility for, local government. In her society she was at the labouring oar, and must have been conscious that no popular movement could exist whose programme offered nothing but negatives. She felt the need of a positive programme, and even announced her intention of using the machinery of the Society for Opposing the Extension of the Parliamentary Suffrage to Women for promoting their activity in Local Government and the election of women to Local Government bodies. But she was sharply pulled up for this by Lord Curzon, who said at a meeting of the society, as reported in the *Anti-suffrage Review :* " The funds we collect are given primarily, *and I think exclusively*, for resistance to the parliamentary vote for women. It is for that purpose, and *that purpose alone*, that our organization exists. . . . I hope you will be quite clear about that." Of course Mrs. Humphry Ward had to give way. Had she not just said at this same meeting " how necessary was the maintenance of the male hand upon the helm of English Government " ? But the male hand of the politician is capable of adaptability to changed circumstances. Lord Curzon, twenty years earlier, had succeeded in reversing the decision of the Royal Geographical Society to elect women as Fellows—an innovation which he then considered "most injurious to men and disastrous to women." Further experience must have convinced him that this injury to men and disaster to women would be a source of strength to the society; for when he found himself in the position of President of the R.G.S., and responsible with others for the increased cost of far larger and more commodious premises, he himself promoted and, I believe, proposed the election of women to the society. Council's opinion was taken, and was to the effect that "on the true construction of the charter and by-laws women were admissible." The noble President therefore had the solace of finding that the law was on his side when he said, "Ay."

The difference between Mrs. Humphry Ward and her chief in 1912 may have been the prototype of the greater difference which divided them in 1918. But at the earlier date it was Mrs. Ward who wished to go forward, and Lord Curzon who resolutely refused to follow; in 1918 the rôles were reversed. It was Lord Curzon who bowed to the inevitable and Mrs. Ward who vehemently protested that the "male hand" had betrayed her.*

We now resume the thread of our story in 1912 after the defeat of the Conciliation Bill by 14 votes on March 28th. One of its results was the change in the election policy of the N.U.W.S.S. described

* See correspondence in the *Morning Post*, January 14th to 21st, 1918.

in the last chapter. Outside of this, our work was concentrated on securing all possible support for the women's suffrage amendments to the Government Franchise Bill. One important advantage was gained when Mr. Redmond gave a definite promise that his party would be left free to vote on women's suffrage according to their personal convictions. The Irish Nationalists, who had in a body deserted the Conciliation Bill, had been very severely criticized for this by their own supporters, both in this country and in Ireland.

The women's suffrage amendments to be moved to the Government Bill were four in number. The first stood in the name of the Foreign Secretary, Sir Edward Grey. It was to delete the word " male " from the first clause. It will be remembered that Mr. Asquith, in the previous July, had said in reference to the Bill, " Whatever extensions of the franchise it makes are to male persons only," and the Bill, therefore, had been drafted in this sense. The deletion of the word " male " from the first clause would not in itself have enfranchised a single woman, but, if accepted by the House, it would have rendered the inclusion of women by amendment a possibility. Three amendments to include women were therefore drafted, representing three degrees of comparison, corresponding, roughly, to the degrees of enthusiasm of different sections of the House for the free citizenship of women.

The first amendment represented the views of the Labour Party, and also corresponded with the aims of practically every suffrage society: it demanded the vote for women on the same terms as men. Under the new franchises contemplated in the Bill this would have enfranchised about ten and a half millions of women. We had little hope that this amendment would be carried, as our belief was that Parliament would not consent to the creation of an electorate in which women decidedly outnumbered men. Mr. Arthur Henderson, Chairman of the Parliamentary Labour Party, undertook to move this amendment. He was a very stanch friend of our movement, and could be relied on to support the other amendments if his own were lost.

The second amendment was to create what was virtually household suffrage for women, and proposed to give the franchise to all women over twenty-five years of age who were householders or wives of householders. It was believed that this amendment would enfranchise about six and a half millions of women. It was to be moved by Mr. (now Sir) W. H. Dickinson, also a very stalwart friend, whose tenacity had been tested on many occasions.

The third amendment, to be moved by the Hon. Alfred Lyttelton if the first and second were lost, was on the lines of the Conciliation Bill, and would have enfranchised women householders only, of

whom it was known there were about one and a half
millions in England and Wales. Committees on
party lines were organized in the House of Commons
in support of these amendments, Mr. Henderson,
Mr. Stephen Walsh, and Mr. Snowden, being
especially active on behalf of the Labour Party;
Mr. Acland, Sir Alfred Mond, the Hon. H. D. Mc-
Laren, and Mr. Dickinson, on behalf of the Liberals;
Lord Robert Cecil, Mr. Goulding, Lord Wolmer,
and Sir W. Bull, on behalf of the Conservatives.
Members of the Government could not join these
committees; but some, such as Sir John Simon,
gave very valuable help and advice. The great
point to aim at was to maintain the unity of the
suffragists in all the parties, and thus to secure a
united vote in support of any suffrage amendment
which recommended itself to the House as a whole.
We therefore endeavoured to obtain promises, in
the event of one amendment being defeated, that
those Members who had preferred it should transfer
their support to the next. The Labour Party,
inside and outside the House, was particularly
firm and outspoken in support of this policy.
" We intend to stand by the women through
thick and thin," said one of their leaders. " I will
fight for them, amendment by amendment, with
all the strength that is in me." The annual congress of the Labour Party backed us up by the
resolution recorded on p. 3. The Trade Union

Congress also adopted a very strong suffrage resolution.

But we soon found the parliamentary air thick with the intrigue and gossip which had succeeded in defeating the Conciliation Bill. Rumours and threats of resignation if any form of women's suffrage were carried were rife. One " Right Honourable gentleman " would take an Irish Nationalist on one side and remark casually that it was lamentable to think, after the long struggle for Home Rule, that it would be destroyed after all by the break up of the Government over women's suffrage. Sir Edward Grey, intending to counteract these rumours, rather intensified them by writing to a suffrage meeting in Glasgow in December indicating that resignation was a game which two could play at, and if anti-suffrage Ministers resigned as a result of the success of one or other of the suffrage amendments, then non-success must equally be followed by the resignation of Ministers like himself pledged to its support.

It has already been noted that the Session of 1912 had begun in January; the Second Reading of the Government Reform Bill had been taken in July; on the reassembling of Parliament for the autumn Session October and November went by with no signs of any further progress with the Bill. It was the constant subject of conversation and discussion in the Lobbies, in the Press, and in general society, and many public meetings were held, but no parliamentary progress was made; and when this state of things continued over the Christmas recess, and the lengthy Session of 1912 was prolonged into 1913, the more experienced of suffragists were asking each other how it could be a physical possibility to pass a controversial measure like a Reform Bill through all its stages in both Houses of Parliament at the tail end of a Session which had already lasted nearly thirteen months.

An influential meeting in support of the more democratic of the suffrage amendments to the Reform Bill had been held in the Opera House in Kingsway on December 4th. Important speeches were made by Mr. F. D. Acland, Sir John Simon leading Liberal women, and others; but the difficulties and confusion inside the House caused by the Prime Minister's statement in the Second Reading debate, that he "could not suppose that the House would so far stultify itself as to reverse the considered judgment it had already arrived at," continued to darken the outlook, particularly by encouraging the rumours of the resignation of anti-suffrage Ministers and the consequent break up of the Administration. It is to be noted that no official contradiction was given to these very prevalent rumours of resignation *until the day before the House expected to go into Committee on the Bill,* January 22nd, 1913. But the *coup de grâce* for the Reform Bill and those who were responsible for it came from an altogether unexpected quarter. Three days, January 24th, 27th, and 28th, had been allotted to the women's suffrage amendments under a special "guillotine" time-table. This stage, however, was never reached, for on January 23rd Mr. Bonar Law asked the Speaker to give a ruling on the point whether the Government's own amendments to the Bill, regarding the occupation franchise for men, would not so far alter the Bill from that which had received a Second Reading in July as to necessitate its withdrawal and reintroduction in an altered form. The implied argument was, " the Bill which the House read a second time in July is not the same Bill which it is now asked to consider in committee." The Speaker replied that though he could not at that stage give a definite ruling, it was, in point of fact, his opinion that the Bill was not the Bill to which the House had assented in July, and he added that there were " other amendments regarding female suffrage which, of course, would make a huge difference in the Bill if they were inserted." The blow to the whole Bill thus foreshadowed fell like a thunder-bolt on the House, and on no portion of it more severely than on the Government, especially on the Prime Minister Ever since May, 1908, when first Mr. Asquith had become Prime Minister, he had given various forecasts and promises about this Bill, and especially on his attitude and that of his Government to women

4

suffrage amendments. Now all these promises
and forecasts were proved to be absolutely worthless,
mere scraps of paper; and this owing to the conduct
of the Bill by the Government itself. Whether the
Speaker's ruling, which was given definitely a day
or two later, was based on the incorrect naming of
the Bill,* or on the fact that in the Second Reading
debate Mr. Asquith had told the House definitely,
" This Bill does not propose to confer the suffrage
on women, and whatever extensions of the franchise
it makes are to male persons only," was never, according to my knowledge, made public. What everybody
knew was that the Government had blundered
badly, that its chief had given promises which by his
own action he was powerless to fulfil, and that the
proposed Reform Bill promised by him in 1908,
1910, and 1911 was a complete fiasco. The new
situation proved to every suffragist that our measure
could never be carried through all its parliamentary
stages unless it was brought forward by a united
Cabinet as a Government measure. The day for
such success as could be attained by a private
Member's Bill was long passed.

A very considerable number of the general public
were under the impression that we had been " had ";
and there were many among suffragists who thought
that a deliberate fraud or trick had been practised

* The Bill was named the Franchise and Registration
Bill, not a Bill to Amend the Representation of the People.

upon us. I never shared this view. The blow was much more a blow to the Government than to the suffrage movement. It did not harm our movement in public opinion. On the contrary, public opinion was with us; the prestige and authority of the Government were lowered; and they did nothing to retrieve their position so far as we were concerned. If the Prime Minister had sent for the representatives of the suffrage societies, the Women's Liberal Federation, and other bodies standing for suffrage which had formed the deputation in November, 1911, and had said, " I have given you promises which it is unfortunately out of my power to fulfil; will you suggest any course which would be a reasonable substitute in fulfilment of my pledges ?" he would have put the onus of the acceptance or rejection of such an offer upon us; but he did nothing of the sort. We asked him to receive us, but he refused to meet us or to hold any communication with us on the subject. His position, therefore, was that his promises remained unredeemed, and he made no effort to redeem them. It is true that he offered parliamentary time for the discussion of a Second Reading of a private Member's Bill. But it needed not to be a Daniel or a Solomon to see that a private Member's Bill, of which seven had passed Second Reading in the last four years, and four of them in 1908, 1909, 1910, and 1911, was no substitute for a place in a Government Bill, which, if adopted by the House, would be regarded by the Government as an integral part of the measure, and defended in all its stages in both Houses of Parliament. We were furiously indignant. If a man who had owed £1,000 suddenly became bankrupt, and declined any meeting with his creditors, but offered them 1,000 gilded cardboard discs, he could not expect this conduct to assuage their indignation or soften their anger against him, for he would first have robbed them and then treated them as if they were children. One of the papers which usually supported the Government put the case thus: " If A and B arrange a deal, and A is unavoidably prevented from delivering the goods for which B bargained, it is not open to A to offer a different class of goods till he has had B's consent to the substitution." We remembered how, when the militant suffragists had said that Mr. Asquith's promises were worthless, Mr. Lloyd George had indignantly and forcibly retaliated that such a doubt was " an imputation of deep dishonour " which he absolutely repudiated. We took pleasure in recalling Dr. Johnson's description of the Duke of Devonshire of his time, and contrasting it with Mr. Asquith, to the latter's disadvantage. "If," said the Doctor of the third Duke, "he had promised you an acorn and none had grown in his woods that year, he would not have contented himself with that excuse; he would have sent to Denmark for it. So unconditional was he in keeping his word, so high his point of honour." If that was the sort of man the

A PLEASURE DEFERRED.

Suffragist : "You've cut my dance !"
Mr. Asquith : "Yes, I know. The fact is the M.C. objected to the pattern of my waistcoat, and I had to go home and change it. But I'll tell you what ! Let me put you down for an extra at our private subscription dance next season !"

(Reproduced by special permission of the Proprietors of *Punch.*)

Punch, February 5, 1913.]

[Facing page 52.

Duke of Devonshire was, it was the sort of man Mr. Asquith was not. The N.U.W.S.S. decided at its council meeting in February, 1913, to take no part in supporting by work in the constituencies or inside the House this private Member's Bill. Our reasons were that we were now convinced that nothing but a Government Bill, backed by a united Cabinet, would be of any practical service to our cause. Of course the N.U.W.S.S. could never, under any circumstances, oppose any Bill which enfranchised any women, few or many; but we took no part whatever in its support. It came on for Second Reading in May, 1913, and met with the defeat to which from the beginning it had been foredoomed.

The last four years had witnessed the steady advance of the suffrage cause. It was now in the forefront of practical politics, and was a question which had led to more than one serious Cabinet crisis, and was capable of making or unmaking Governments. We held steadfastly to our resolution to work for nothing in Parliament but a Government measure backed by a united Cabinet. Our chief practical consideration was how to do this on constitutional lines and by non-party means. Our friend and colleague, Mrs. Harley, suggested what we afterwards called " The Pilgrimage," and her idea was taken up and carried out with enthusiasm by the whole National Union. An account of the Pilgrimage will form the subject of the next chapter.

CHAPTER V

THE PILGRIMAGE AND THE DERBY DAY, 1913

" Proclaim liberty throughout the land unto all the inhabitants thereof."—LEV. xxv. 10

THE Pilgrimage was a piece of work which could only have been undertaken successfully by a powerful organization, and such the N.U.W.S.S. certainly was. We had divided the whole area of Great Britain into nineteen federations; in each federation there was a working committee meeting regularly, whose aim was to form a non-militant, non-party women's suffrage society in every parliamentary borough in its area. Each federation and each society aimed at being self-supporting; but the large sums, amounting to many thousands of pounds, collected at our big Albert Hall demonstrations in London enabled the executive committee of the whole N.U.W.S.S. to make grants for special work to specified societies or federations. Our organization was thoroughly democratic, the executive committee and all the officers being subject to election at our annual council meetings, where each society could claim representation in proportion

54

to its numbers. No new departure in policy could
be undertaken without the authority of the council.
In 1913 we had over 400 societies, and they were
constantly increasing; in 1914, just before the
war, there were over 600. We calculated that,
adding together the central funds, the Election
Fighting Fund, and the funds raised and expended
by our societies locally, the National Union at this
time was using over £45,000 a year for the further-
ance of the enfranchisement of women.

We were giving full time employment to scores
of organizers, mostly highly intelligent young women
of University education, who not only did admirable
propaganda work throughout the country, but
kept headquarters informed of all important local
developments and incidents bearing on our movement.

The Pilgrimage was a march of bands of our
societies, all non-militant suffragists, from every
part of Great Britain, converging on London, and
so arranged as to reach their goal on the same day.
Eight routes were selected: the great North Road,
the Fen Country, the East Coast, Watling Street,
the West Country Road, the Portsmouth Road,
the Brighton Road, and the Kentish Pilgrims' Way.
In each case the Pilgrimage procession started at
the point most distant from London, carrying
banners, and accompanied, where possible, by
music. The pilgrims were prepared to stop and

hold meetings, distribute literature, and collect
funds in towns and villages *en route*. As they
proceeded their numbers rolled up; friends lent
motor-cars for conveying luggage, and the most
wonderfully generous hospitality was extended to
them all along the route, especially in the towns
where we had powerful societies. This we might
have been said to expect; but what surprised us was
the extraordinarily warm welcome we received from
the villages we passed through. Once their inhabitants understood that we were non-militant, and
had no desire to injure anybody or anything, they
gave us the most cordial reception; indeed, we
were often stopped as we were passing through
villages which we had deemed hardly large enough
for a meeting with the remonstrance, " You are
surely never going to pass us by without saying a
word !"

The meetings in the towns were not so uniformly
friendly. Hooligans sometimes declined to believe
that we were non-militant, and demonstrated their
enthusiasm for law and order by throwing dead rats,
potatoes, rotten eggs, and other garbage, at our
speakers. No real harm was done to any of us, but
occasionally the services of the police were needed
to protect our speakers. This, however, was exceptional, and had reactions in our favour. For instance,
one lady, well on her way towards old age, who had
started on our Pilgrimage at Land's End, originally

intended to break off her march at Plymouth, but, being roughly treated by a band of disorderly youths at Camborne, resolved that she would accompany the pilgrims all the way to London, which she did. The start was made in each case from the points most distant from London on June 18th, and the Pilgrimage in all its eight branches arrived in London on July 25th, the final demonstration being held in Hyde Park on July 26th. Here there were nineteen platforms, representing the nineteen federations of the N.U.W.S.S. There was a huge and an entirely sympathetic crowd in the Park. When a bugle sounding from the central platform announced the putting of the resolution, there was hardly a hand held up against it.

On the next day—Sunday, July 27th—many hundreds of the pilgrims, wearing their badges and colours, assembled in Trafalgar Square and walked in procession, but without banners, to St. Paul's to attend the afternoon service. A large number of seats had been courteously reserved for them under the dome, and a sermon appropriate to the occasion was preached by Canon Simpson. We thought it just like our good luck that the first Psalm for the evening service on the twenty-seventh day of the month was the absolutely appropriate one: " When the Lord turned again the captivity of Sion, then were we like unto them that dream. . . . They that sow in tears shall reap in joy. He that goeth

on his way weeping, and bearing forth good seed,
shall doubtless come again with joy, and bring his
sheaves with him." A deep sense of peace and of
absolute confidence in our ultimate triumph came
upon us. We were as certain of it as if it had already
been in our grasp.

It may not be inappropriate here to add a few
words about Mrs. Harley, who originated the
Pilgrimage. She was a woman of great originality
and imagination. The widow of a soldier, and sister
of General French, she had lived most of her life
among military people and in a military atmosphere.
She was the life and soul of the suffrage movement
in Shrewsbury and the neighbourhood, where her
fine character has left a lasting impression. In
December, 1914, she joined the first unit of the
Scottish Women's Hospitals for foreign service under
Dr. Elsie Inglis, and acted as administrator of the
great hospital, afterwards so famous, which was
opened in the Abbaye de Royaumont. Mrs. Harley
took her young daughter with her as one of her
orderlies. On one occasion, when this gently
nurtured girl was scrubbing a ward, a sick French
soldier asked her if it were true that she was the
niece of Lord French. When she replied in the
affirmative, the poilu rejoined: " I don't think
General Joffre's niece would scrub our ward." These
little things made a deep impression, and, I am told,
puzzled our French friends not a little. When the

French Government asked the S.W.H. for a second hospital, one was opened at Troyes, and Mrs. Harley accompanied it, again acting as administrator. It was the first open-air hospital ever seen in France. The soldiers nursed in it were enthusiastic in their praise. When the French Expeditionary Force was sent to Salonica the French Government asked the Scottish Women's Hospitals Committee to allow this unit to go with it, a request which was, of course, willingly granted. While at Salonica Mrs. Harley received from the French military authorities the Croix de Guerre avec Palme, a decoration which she brought to show us at our suffrage office in the summer of 1916, when she was in London for a short time arranging for the transport to Serbia of a couple of motor ambulances. This was the last time we saw her, for she was killed by Bulgarian shell-fire at Monastir on March 7th, 1917. Her works do follow her. A very fine tribute to her memory was paid by the Serbian authorities on the occasion of the unveiling of a memorial to her. " To die for one's country," said one of the Serbs, " that is fine, but that we understand; but to die for another country, that is superb—that is something beyond us."

Returning to the Pilgrimage and its results. Petitions to Parliament in favour of women's suffrage had been sent up from the very numerous meetings which the pilgrims had held while on their march towards London. These were presented by our friends in the House in batches, with short speeches, not just dropped silently into the bag behind the Speaker's chair, as in the old days. A number of M.P.'s received deputations from their constituents who had taken part in the Pilgrimage. At the end of July the Home Secretary, Mr. McKenna, received a deputation from some of the pilgrims, who wished to bring to his notice the inadequacy of police protection given at some of the meetings they had addressed. One of the speakers said there was an impression abroad that women's suffrage meetings were fair game, and that disorder and hooliganism could take place at these without disagreeable consequences to those who indulged in them. In his reply there was a notable change for the better in Mr. McKenna's attitude towards the N.U.W.S.S. He asked for a list of the meetings of which complaint was made, and promised enquiry, adding that he would do his utmost to give suffragists protection as complete as that extended to other citizens holding peaceful political meetings. He even added: " I sincerely admire the courage with which you have carried on your work . . . and I honestly believe that your method of action has assisted your cause." This was a great improvement compared with the time, not many months earlier, when he was so long in making up his mind whether or not to prosecute us for promo ing the sale of an " obscene " book.

The Pilgrimage also led to a deputation from the N.U.W.S.S. being received by Mr. Asquith. We noted, too, in his attitude and language a notable improvement; we felt that his education in the principles of representative government was progressing. Mrs. Harley, Miss Margaret Robertson, Mrs. Rackham, and Miss Royden spoke chiefly of the widespread interest in and sympathy with our movement which had been demonstrated during the Pilgrimage. It fell to me, as leader of the deputation, to try to wring from him some acknowledgment that he had not fulfilled the pledges he had given the suffrage deputation in November, 1911. I reminded him of these pledges, and maintained that they had not been fulfilled, and reviewed the series of events which had led suffragists to the unanimous conclusion that the only way in which their fulfilment was now possible was by means of a Government Bill. I reminded Mr. Asquith that several of his colleagues had repeatedly assured us that the opportunity offered them by him in November, 1911, was far better than any chances afforded by a private Member's Bill. Mr. Asquith at this point interjected, " So they were. It was the truth." This enabled me again to emphasize our main point—namely, that the offer of time for a private Member's Bill was a totally inadequate substitute for what we had lost by the Government's mishandling of their own measure. Proceeding, I recalled two comparatively modern instances in which Liberal Governments had been divided on the question of franchise reform.   Lord Palmerston, leader of the Liberals in the early sixties, opposed the extension of the franchise to working men just as Mr. Asquith now opposed its extension to women.   The result was that it was left to a Conservative Government to carry the needed reform.   Lord Goschen, in 1880, had stood aside from active participation in party politics because of his opposition to the enfranchisement of the agricultural labourer.   I pressed Mr. Asquith to follow the example of Lord Goschen rather than that of Lord Palmerston, and not to allow his own views to stand in the way of what he himself had acknowledged to be the desire of the majority of his colleagues in the Government and the House of Commons.   Finally, I urged him not to shut his eyes to the fact that the women's demand to share in self-government was a vital and living movement, a development of the basic principle of democracy, and was founded on the growth of education and the wider industrial and professional opportunities which women had won for themselves during the last two generations.   " We have ceased to have the serf's mind and the serf's economic helplessness, and it follows that the serf's political status no longer contents us.   The Government is now meeting the demand of women for free institutions with coercion, and nothing but coercion·

It is not thus that the victories of Liberalism have been won. I readily admit that the maintenance of order is one of the first duties of every Government. But another is to redress the grievances from which disorder has sprung."

In reply, Mr. Asquith confessed himself to have been greatly impressed by the Pilgrimage and its reception in the country; but though he admitted that we were in a position of great hardship, and virtually acknowledged that what he had offered us in January, 1913, was no equivalent for what he had promised us in November, 1911, he declined to say what steps his Government were prepared to take in the future on the suffrage question. But he said: " Proceed as you have been proceeding. Continue to the end;" and that it would be quite impossible for a minority in the Liberal Party to obstruct or prevent the realization of our hopes. Parliament would yield, as it had always hitherto done, and as it was bound to do, to the opinion of the country . . . it was a matter which in the final resort must be decided by the people themselves. Asked how he expected the judgment of the people to express itself, Mr. Asquith replied: " I think, in the long run, there is only one way of finding out what people think, and that is by an election." But under present conditions, as we did not fail to remind him, those most concerned in the present matter would not possess one single vote. Members of the Government favourable to women's suffrage also received a deputation from the N.U.W.S.S. on the same day. The interview was private, but when members of both deputations compared notes, we agreed that the antisuffrage Prime Minister was less discouraging than his prosuffrage colleagues. They plentifully douched us with cold water. Only one of them, Sir John Simon, made any helpful suggestion.

One part of the remarks made by me to the Prime Minister seems to call for some further explanation: it is that in which I had referred to the existence of disorder, and that the Government's one and only remedy for disorder was coercion, and again coercion, ever more and more harshly and relentlessly applied, unaccompanied by any statesmanlike effort to redress the grievances from which disorder had sprung. This, of course, had reference to militantism, which was at its height in 1913. Liberals all over the country were quite willing to endorse John Bright's wise saying, " Force is no remedy "; but they seemed absolutely incapable of finding the real remedy— the extension to women of free institutions. Mr. Asquith had proclaimed that the object of his Government was " to set upon an unshakable foundation the principles of Representative Government," while maintaining that its application to women would be a political mistake of a disastrous nature. Quite recently, at a Lord Mayor's banquet, he had referred with well-founded complacency to the rapid reconciliation of the Boer population of South Africa, and had exclaimed, " Great is the magic of free institutions !" What we demanded was not the repetition of these mouth-filling phrases, but their application in our own case. The N.U.W.S.S. had consistently and persistently opposed militantism from the moment when the so-called militants attempted to promote their political aims by the use of personal violence. At the outset they had suffered violence, but used none; but this policy had, from 1908 onwards, been abandoned, and they openly took up the weapon of physical force, and in retaliation physical force was used against them brutally and unscrupulously. Forcible feeding, the Cat and Mouse Act, were the weapons of the Government. " Frightfulness " in the German sense had been used on both sides, and the frightfulness of the Government was as sincerely deprecated by all of us as the frightfulness of the militants. Again and again, on all possible occasions, we urged that the redress of grievances was the true remedy for disorder. We recognized, along with very large numbers of people hitherto uninterested in our movement, the courage and power of self-sacrifice of the militants, but we felt that the use of the weapon of physical force was the negation of the very principle for which we struggled ; it was d nying our faith to make our faith prevail.

In the early summer of 1913 an incident occurred which deeply touched the popular imagination, and placed the principle of self-sacrifice as illustrated by the militants on a hill-top from which it was seen not only all over our own country, but throughout the world. Courage calls to courage everywhere, and its voice cannot be denied.

The race for the Derby was held on the last Wednesday of May. The King's horse was the favourite. Crowds even more enormous than usual gathered to witness it; among them a young woman, a militant suffragist, Emily Davidson, of Morpeth, in Northumberland, had managed to place herself close to the winning-post against the rope barrier which kept the crowd off the actual track. As the King's horse swept by at a tremendous speed, Emily Davidson threw herself in front of it. Down came the horse with fearful violence; the jockey was, of course, thrown, and seriously injured; and there lay Emily Davidson, mortally injured. She had deliberately sacrificed her life in order, in this sensational way, to draw the attention of the whole world to the determination of women to share in the heritage of freedom which was the boast of every man in the country. The King enquired for the jockey; the Queen enquired for the injured woman In a day or two it was announced that she was dead She never recovered consciousness. She had died for her cause. After one of the military disasters which accompanied the early development of the Risorgimento in Italy, the historian writes that young Italy had, at least, shown that it knew how to die. Emily Davidson had shown that she, too, knew how to die. I happened to be in Vienna at the time and I shall not easily forget the awed solemnity with which a Viennese with whom I had had some halting conversation in German on the suffrage question came to me and said, " Miss Davidson ist todt."

It is said that the urgency of the suffrage problem in Great Britain was one reason which induced the ex-Kaiser and his advisers to consider England a decadent power; if this is true, it is only an example of the way in which he misread every sign of the times and totally misunderstood this country. That a woman was capable of throwing away her life on the chance that it might serve the cause of freedom might have taught him to expect what happened about fourteen months later, when over 5,000,000 young Englishmen voluntarily joined the army in order to preserve the principles of liberty and self-government throughout the world.

CHAPTER VI

THE TURN OF THE TIDE

" Yet die not: do thou
Wear rather in thy bonds a cheerful brow.
Live and take comfort. . . . Thou hast great allies."

AFTER the Pilgrimage, but whether because of it or not we could not judge, we began to receive much more general support from the public and from the Press than ever before. This process was prob_ ably accelerated by the character of some of the legislation which had recently passed through Parliament. The National Insurance Act, for instance, in 1912, caused a great stir, some of it extremely nonsensical, such as a huge meeting got up mainly by antisuffrage women to protest that they would perish rather than stick the insurance stamps on their servants' policies. The Society for Opposing the Extension of the Parliamentary Suffrage to Women, however, presented to Mr. Lloyd George a really excellent memorial on the subject of the Insurance Bill as it affected women, in the course of which they asked whether it would not be better if the Bill provided for women the kind of insurance they wanted rather than the kind which they did not want. We suffragists, of course, did not fail to point the moral that the way to get the legislation women wanted was to let women have votes. Mr. Lloyd George, who had charge of the Bill throughout, was, however, very accessible to suggestions about it, and received deputations in which women of all kinds took part, mistresses and maids, as well as women in industrial occupations. He said he had learnt much from them, and that their point of view had not occurred to him before he had had the opportunity of meeting them. The suffragists again were not slow to point the moral: If women had been voters, their point of view would have been ascertained and considered from the outset.

One almost ludicrous feature of the Insurance Bill as it first passed through Parliament was the payment of the maternity benefit granted under it to the father and not to the mother. One of our Conservative supporters, Mr. R. Prothero (now Lord Ernle), said, in reference to this: " It is a small detail. But it is impossible to imagine that a Parliament elected by women would have allowed the maternity benefit to be paid to the husband, and would have given the woman the remedy of prosecuting the man, with whom she must continue to live, if he does not spend it properly." The improper use of the maternity benefit by the husband probably was quite exceptional; but there were cases known in which the husband had spent it in the public-house or to buy himself a gramophone; and in such cases it was poor comfort to the wife to tell her that she could protect herself by prosecuting her husband, and get him fined or sent to prison.

As far as argument was concerned our battle was won. The antisuffragists, when they pulled themselves together sufficiently to have a great meeting, continually fell back, even in the case of their more distinguished speakers, on the undeniable statement that men were men, and women were women. Another speaker at the Albert Hall antisuffrage meeting gravely reproached the suffragists for wilfully misleading industrial women by persuading them that women's wages would be favourably affected by the possession of political power. His words were: " It is a heartless and cruel deception to tell poor women that the possession of a vote would enable them to raise their wages. Parliament has never attempted such a thing for men." This was on February 28th, 1912. Within less than a month the Government, of which he remained a member, did regulate the minimum rate of wages for men and boys in coal-mines. We believed that the triumph of the miners was in part due to their electoral power.

The antisuffragists were greatly elated by the success of their Albert Hall meeting, and their monthly organ, *The Antisuffrage Review*, for March

triumphantly exclaimed: " The great demonstration
has been held, and the woman's suffrage bubble
has been pricked." Mrs. Humphry Ward, however,
took a different and a more subdued line. Speaking
at Oxford a little later, she said that "the real fight
was only beginning, and would probably last a long
time." As pricked bubbles are not of a very durable
character, she thus virtually disowned the exuberant
metaphor of her paper. But the small fry in the
antisuffrage movement were about this time more
than usually offensive and inept. One of them, a
woman writer with a tolerably well-known name,
published the following: " For social purposes, now
and always, man is superior to woman. Organized
society rests on him. It would go on quite com-
fortably if every woman retired to her own particular
wigwam and did nothing but breed." Another
writer, probably male, not to be left behind in
offensive rubbish, wrote in the *Liverpool Courier*:
" Votes for women ! Why, the matter is in a nut-
shell. If married, she exercises the franchise through
her husband. If a widow, she is a past-partner in a
joint concern, and should rest content with the
achievement of other days. If single, she is, or
ought to be, too busily engaged in trying to capture
' John Henry Charles ' to think about votes." De-
grading and vulgar nonsense of this kind was nauseat-
ing to every decent-minded man or woman, whether
for or against suffrage; but it made many who had

previously been indifferent turn with sympathy to those who were claiming political freedom for women and trying to preach and live the gospel of a nobler and truer relationship between the sexes.

> "Self-reverent each and reverencing each,
> Distinct in individualities,
> But like each other ev'n as those who love."

These coarse and foolish attacks upon our whole movement did it not one ounce of harm.

It was in the spring of 1914 that Lord Selborne raised the question of women's suffrage in the House of Lords. It was the first time that suffrage ground had been broken in any serious sense in the Upper Chamber. A Bill was introduced on the lines of the Conciliation Bill, and came on for Second Reading on May 5th. Eleven peers spoke in its favour, and seven in opposition. Among the speeches on our side Lord Lytton's rose to the level of the very highest excellence. The House, so proverbially difficult to move in any emotional sense, was obviously and deeply moved by his earnestness, transparent sincerity, and closely reasoned argument. Gossip said that as he concluded Lord Curzon threw himself back in his seat and exclaimed, *sotto voce*, to his next neighbour: "' What a tragedy that such talent should be wasted upon women !" Another peer who took the anti-suffrage side, and used language comparable to the specimens quoted on the previous page, caused an old-fashioned country gentleman type of antisuffrage peer sitting on the Conservative side to exclaim: "I shall go. If I listen to this fellow any longer I should be driven to vote for the Bill." Lord Curzon moved its rejection, and it was defeated by 104 votes to 60. The suffragists were more than gratified by this result, and by the debate and the general reception given to the subject.

A number of other things were happening month by month which indicated the growing strength of our movement. The Labour Party, preparing its programme for the next General Election, placed in the forefront of its demands " a Government Reform Bill, which must include the enfranchisement of women." Within the Women's Liberal Federation a Liberal Women's Suffrage Union was formed, pledging its members to undertake no work in support of antisuffrage Liberal candidates. A Liberal Men's Association for Women's Suffrage was also formed, under the chairmanship of Mr. W. Barton, M.P. for Oldham. Mr. Barton had recently claimed the right of Liberal women in his constituency to attend a party meeting to be addressed by Mr. Asquith, and this not as guests accompanying the speakers, but as political workers in the constituency. The extraordinary attitude adopted by many Liberal Associations towards women at this time may be gauged by the fact that Mr. Barton had to threaten to resign his seat before he could induce the Oldham Liberal Association to admit women Liberals to their meeting.

Contemporaneously with this, women's suffrage was making way within the Conservative Party. At the annual conference of the National Conservative and Unionist Associations at Norwich, Lord Robert Cecil moved " that it is expedient to extend the franchise to all citizens, regardless of sex, who have the qualifications at present required of men for the exercise of the suffrage." The opponents did not venture on a direct negative, but moved " that it is not expedient to grant the parliamentary franchise to women on any terms until this great constitutional change has received the express sanction of the electors." This amendment was carried by a large majority; but Lord Robert Cecil had made a deep impression on the association in connection with this and other subjects debated by them, and his present very leading position in politics was from this date distinctly indicated.

Support for suffrage came at this time from another and a much less expected quarter. The Ulster Unionist Council in September, 1913, approved the draft articles of the Ulster Provincial Government which it was intended to set up in the event of the Home Rule Act coming into operation, and these articles embodied the enfranchisement of women on the basis of the Local Government register.   Indeed, the Ulster Unionist Council went further than this. For, writing to the Ulster Women's Unionist Association, the secretary of the U.U. Council asked for " names of women willing to act upon the various committees which will on that date (the date of the creation of a Nationalist Parliament) be established. This ensures that those who have so heartily supported us in the past will immediately be co-opted with a view to taking their proper share in the management of the affairs of Ulster whilst we are holding the province on trust for the British nation, in which matter we fully realize that their interests are as much at stake as those of the men."

This attitude on the part of the Ulster Unionist Council was all the more satisfactory to us because up to that time we had reason to believe Sir Edward Carson to be among our most determined opponents.

About the same time the Church Congress, meeting in Southampton under the presidency of the Bishop of Winchester, arranged a debate on the Ideals of Manhood and Womanhood. The Bishop ruled that the political aspects of the subject would not be out of order. Miss Royden spoke, and made so deep an impression that her speech was referred to a year later by the Bishop of Lichfield, preaching in Hull, "as the epoch-making address of Miss Maude Royden." The Bishop of Winchester wrote to the Press, replying to attacks made upon him in defence of his attitude on women's suffrage at the Church Congress. He pleaded for truce and amnesty between the Government and the suffrage party, and urged as a necessary preliminary to this the definite prospect of the introduction by the Government of a Women's Suffrage Bill as a first-class measure. From that meeting of the Church Congress at Southampton dates, I believe, the very strong and undivided support given to our movement by the Bishops in the House of Lords.

We also had evidence at this time of the support of another religious body, the Society of Friends, who this year, in their *Annual Epistle*, issued from the London yearly meeting, made a very sympathetic reference to the women's movement. We valued this all the more because of their fine record in the matter of sex equality in religious matters from the foundation of their society. They had from the first practised as well as preached the doctrine of equality as between men and women, and had again and again been pioneers in matters of education and social reform, besides giving us many of our most valued colleagues and leaders.

In 1913 also the National Union of Women Workers (now the National Council of Women) had the last of a series of tussles with Mrs. Humphry Ward. The point at issue between the suffragists and antisuffragists in the N.U.W.W was the necessary majority required on any particular subject before the executive committee was justified in taking action upon it. A committee for revising the constitution had been at work, and had presented a report recommending, among other things, that no action should be taken on any controversial point unless such action were supported by a three-fourths majority; this was by way of an olive-branch, as the necessary majority under the old constitution had been one of two-thirds. To this proposed compromise the antisuffragists presented a solid opposition. Some desired that the council should be deprived of the power of passing resolutions at all. Mrs. Ward proposed that no resolution should be binding unless passed unanimously— a reminiscence, apparently, of the *liberum veto* which contributed so much to the ruin of the old Polish Constitution. Driven from this position' she then proposed to give to any five branches and five affiliated societies an absolute veto upon the proceedings of the council. In each of these efforts Mrs. Ward was unsuccessful, and in a gathering of over 400 she could not rally sufficient votes to carry any of her points. The Antisuffrage Society in consequence withdrew from the N.U.W.W., and figuratively shook its dust from their feet.

At the opening of this chapter I referred to the more favourable tone in the Press upon women's suffrage and allied questions. For quite a number of years we had had true and faithful friends in the *Manchester Guardian*, the *Aberdeen Free*

Press, and in *Punch*, and other papers. The latter gave us a series of first-rate pictures and cartoons, which I hope one day may be reproduced as *Punch's* " History of Women's Suffrage." Its occasional verses were also very crisp and to the point. A couple of specimens are here reproduced. The first was apropos of Mr. Asquith's frequent statement in the course of his struggle with the House of Lords that " the will of the people must prevail."

> " You speak, Mr. Asquith, the suffragist said,
>   Of the Will of the People wholesale,
> But has the idea never entered your head
>   That the People are not wholly male ? "

Another, which was headed " Any Premier to any Suffragist," ran thus:

> " So, lady, it is plain,
>   While at your claim one man shies,
> Until you have the vote tis vain
>   To ask us for the franchise."

About this time the editor of the *Daily Telegraph* allotted space in his paper once a week, under the heading of " Women in Public Life," for the discussion of all kinds of women's activities, including suffrage. It also gave good telegraphic summaries of events bearing on the women's cause in foreign countries, and sometimes even printed the speeches of suffrage leaders verbatim. As our struggle for

suffrage became more and more a struggle with
Mr. Asquith it not unnaturally followed that those
papers were naturally estranged from us which lived,
and moved, and had their being in believing that he
was the first of men, and that everything he said
and did was perfect. They did not go back definitely, and in so many words, upon their former
record in support of free representative institutions,
but they gave us many a back-hander, published
everything conspicuously which they thought likely
to be damaging to us, and suppressed such events
as told in our favour. I give an instance. In a copy
of an evening paper in 1913 I saw in one column,
apropos of some House of Commons incident, that
" Mrs. Fawcett was in despair "; in another that
" Mr. Birrell had finished with women's suffrage
for ever "; and that " Mr. Wilfred Ashley had felt
compelled to vote against it." As I knew I was not
in despair, and had never given any justification
for the assertion that I was, I contemplated with
some calm the assertions about Mr. Birrell and Mr.
Ashley. We did not complain of this sort of treatment. The tactics it revealed were too transparent
to do our movement any real harm. The papers
which we familiarly referred to as " the three *Posts* "
—the *Morning Post*, the *Birmingham Post*, and the
Yorkshire Post—remained out-and-out antisuffrage
all through down to the very end of our struggle.
But the *Standard*, which at one time had refused

even to insert colourless paragraphs of suffrage news, passed to new editorship, and became much more favourable. It referred sympathetically to our by-election campaigns in 1912 and 1913, saying that suffragists " were displaying energy of the first order "; and after the procession in the Coronation year, which had attracted much favourable notice, it arranged for the daily appearance of a special page, entitled " Woman's Platform," in which facts and arguments for and against suffrage were inserted. This was of great use to us, and we welcomed the publication of the antisuffrage copy, because this gave the paper an entry into the strongholds of our opponents, and also enabled us to judge of their policy and tactics. For instance, it was in the " Woman's Platform " of the *Standard*, in 1913, that Mr. MacCallum Scott called upon his Liberal friends in the House of Commons to break their suffrage pledges in order to save Mr. Asquith from the humiliation of keeping the promises he had made to us.

In 1913 the Conservative and Unionist Women's Franchise Association, of which the Countess of Selborne had become President, had the happy thought of instituting through the medium of a joint committee of suffragists and antisuffragists a systematic and careful enquiry into the results of women's suffrage in those States of the U.S.A. where it had been put into operation. A *question-*

naire was drawn up and sent to men and women occupying positions of authority and influence in these States. Of the sixty-three replies received, forty-six were wholly favourable, eight neutral, five vaguely unfavourable, and only four wholly adverse.

The late Hon. Robert Palmer, Lady Selborne's son, tabulated the replies, and published an explanatory comment on them from the suffrage point of view, while the same task on behalf of the anti-suffragists was performed by Mr. MacCallum Scott, M.P.

Both reports appeared in the form of articles in the *Nineteenth Century and After* of February, 1914. Mr. Palmer's article was later published as a small volume, and formed a valuable handbook for suffrage speakers. The supporters of suffrage in the U.S.A. frequently expressed themselves as convinced by experience that the women voters strengthened the forces which made for good government, using such expressions as this: " I do not think we could have cleaned up the city without the women's vote "; or, " At that time I was opposed to wom n suffrage . . . but since I have had experience of it I have become favourable." Mr. MacCallum Scott did not, of course, deny that by an immense majority the replies had supported the women's vote, or that it had been followed, in California, for example, by the immediate passing of much long-sought-for social legislation; but he concluded his article with

6

the words: " I have tried to sum up the evidence as impartially as possible, but I have not tried to conceal my own views, and I have found nothing in the evidence to modify them."

Another very significant breach in the anti-suffragist Press stronghold was revealed when on the last day of 1913 *The Times* published one of its American Supplements " On the Pacific Coast," and, to the amazement and joy of suffragists, wrote most warmly in praise of the complete success of women's suffrage on the whole Pacific seaboard. Suffragists had won the State of Washington in 1910, California in 1911, Oregon and Arizona in 1912. We had expected nothing from *The Times* but flouts, and gibes, and sneers, and lo ! it blessed us altogether. The concluding paragraph sufficiently indicates the general character of the article. It ran thus:

" One-fifth of the United States Senate, one-seventh of the House of Representatives, and one-sixth of the Presidential electoral vote of the United States comes now from States where women exercise suffrage just as men do. Homes have not been disrupted, marriages have not lessened, children have not failed because of the political enfranchisement of women. Instead, there has come a more solemn feeling of obligation, a greater feeling of responsibility on the part of men and women, a higher moral tone in candidates and in measures, and an effort to make the city streets and the country at large a safer place for children when they leave the precincts where maternal love reigns supreme. The women of the suffrage States care not only for their own children, but for the children of women not so fortunately placed."

What a change this represented from the time, three years earlier when every day for nearly a fortnight *The Times* in its leading articles and correspondence columns fulminated on the unmeasured national misfortunes which must necessarily result from the enfranchisement of women.

Immediately all our group wrote for as many copies of this blessed supplement as our newsagents could supply. The stock from this source was quickly exhausted; then I wrote officially to *The Times* office, asking for more, only to receive the reply that no more copies could be obtained. Then we applied for leave to reprint, but the request was declined on the ground that it was the intention of the management to publish the whole supplement in book form. On enquiring the probable date and price, the first question was unanswered, and the reply to the second mentioned what we considered a prohibitive sum.

But we never saw that book. Of course, I carefully preserved my own copy, and quoted it continually when I was speaking. The evidence it gave coincided entirely with what we had learned from our American friends at the Congress of the International Women's Suffrage Alliance held the previous June at Buda Pest, when ladies from the newly enfranchised State of California had told us that, after winning the vote, they had gained in six months legislative reforms for which (without the vote) they had been labouring in vain for twenty years. Twenty months of suffrage, our American friends told us, were worth more than twenty years of " influence."

Another of the signs of the great progress of our cause was the continual increase of the support given to it in modern drama. At this time nearly all the really telling plays by up-to-date writers were practically suffrage plays. Some—like *How the Vote was Won*, by Miss Cecily Hamilton; *Votes for Women*, by Miss Elizabeth Robins; and *Press Cuttings*, by Mr. Bernard Shaw—were propaganda plays pure and simple, and very good propaganda, too, extremely witty and amusing. Others, even more telling because a good deal more subtle in method, were by Sir James Barrie, Mr. Arnold Bennett, and many by Mr. Bernard Shaw. These were of very great service to our cause, as well as a sign of its progress; while the plays on the moral aspects of our movement, such as *Les Trois Filles de M. Dupont* and *Les Avariés*, by M. Brieux, brought our message to thousands whom we could not have reached unaided

No wonder that, with all the influences enumerated in this chapter working in our favour, we felt we were on the eve of victory. We quoted, with an application to ourselves, Cavour's prophetic saying,

" La cosa va." Seldom has a political movement
had such a various army of allies: the Trades Union
Congress, the Labour Party, the Church Congress,
the annual meeting of the Society of Friends, the
Ulster Unionist Council, the Press, the Pulpit, and
the Theatre. But a great catastrophe was at hand,
which for four and a half years concentrated all
thoughts on national safety, and, above all, on the
preservation of the principles of free representative
government, not merely in our own country, but
throughout the world.

CHAPTER VII

THE WORLD WAR AND WOMEN'S WAR WORK

" What have I done for you,
England, my England ?
What is there I would not do,
England, my own ?
With your glorious eyes austere,
As if the Lord were walking near,
Whispering terrible things and dear
As the song on your bugles blown,
England—
Round the world on your bugles blown."
W. E. HENLEY.

IN the midst of all the plans of organized work detailed in previous chapters, which were certain, as we thought, to lead to speedy victory for the suffrage cause, we were suddenly startled by the trumpet call of war, the world war, the greatest which ever had been waged, and our own country was to be a protagonist in it. The wanton violation of Belgium neutrality by the Germans made this a certainty. Very soon, too, we realized how right the socialists of the allied countries—England, France, Belgium, and Russia—were when they agreed that " a victory for German Imperialism would be the defeat and destruction of democracy and liberty in Europe," and we recognized that our cause, the political freedom of women, was but a special case of the still greater cause for which the Allies were fighting. Clearly as we began to perceive this, it will easily be recognized that the time of the outbreak of war was a time of no little perplexity and anguish of mind to nearly all of us. But from the first our duty was quite clear—namely, to help our country and her allies to the utmost of our ability; many of us, however, myself included, believed that the great catastrophe of the world war would greatly hamper and retard the movement to which we had dedicated our lives. It only very gradually dawned upon us that one of the first results of the war would be the emancipation of women in our own and many other countries.

It will be remembered that England entered the war against Germany at midnight on Tuesday, August 4th, 1914. All that day and the previous day the Executive Committee of the N.U.W.S.S. had sat in anxious consultation. We were a tolerably large band of organized women—over 50,000 members, and about 500 societies—scattered all over the country, accustomed to work together in a disciplined, orderly fashion for a common end; we felt, therefore, that we had a special gift, such as it was, to offer for our country's service—namely, our organizing and money-raising power.

In my first message to our societies, published in the *Common Cause* on August 7th, 1914, I had said:

" In the midst of this time of terrible anxiety and grief, it is some little comfort to think that our large organization, which has been carefully built up during past years to promote women's suffrage, can be used now to help our country through this period of strain and sorrow. ' He that findeth his life shall lose it, and he that loseth his life for My sake shall find it.' Let us show ourselves worthy of citizenship, whether our claim to it be recognized or not."

In the ordinary course of things we could not by the rules of our union have made any change in our methods of work, and still less have applied our organization to any other object than the gaining of the parliamentary franchise for women, without calling our council together and receiving its express authorization. The circumstances of the hour rendered this impossible, and we took the only available alternative: we consulted our societies by post. Even this was not quite simple, as a large number of the officers of our societies were scattered, at the beginning of August, in various holiday resorts. However, it was the best we could do, and the Executive Committee intimated to all the societies its opinion that the ordinary political work of the union and all propaganda must be suspended; and that the best way of using our staff and organizing capacity would be in initiating forms of work

designed to mitigate the suffering which the war
would bring.

The alleviation of distress among women caused
by the dislocation of employment due to the war
was our first object. When events rendered efforts
in this direction no longer necessary, we enlarged the
scope of our activities so as to include everything
that was calculated to "sustain the vital energies
of the nation." But the preliminary necessity in
that first week of the war was to know that we had
the backing of our societies throughout the country.
We had consulted them by post on August 3rd,
and we met again on August 6th to consider the
replies received. Ninety-nine per cent. of these
acquiesced in our suggestion. Two of them contained sketch plans of methods of work on the new
lines. We concentrated at first on using our whole
organization for the relief of distress caused by the
war. We suggested to each of our societies that it
should formally offer the services of its officers and
members to the Lord Mayor, Mayor, or Chairman
of the Council in its own district, and should volun
teer to take part in the local relief committees which
were being formed in every local government area
under directions issued by the Local Government
Board. Like almost everyone else in those troubled,
anxious times, we expected that there would be a
great deal of distress owing to unemployment;
and there was temporarily great dislocation of indus-

try and lack of work, especially among women. On August 27th, 1914, we unanimously adopted a resolution, moved and seconded by our hon. secretary and hon. parliamentary secretary, urging the Government, long before anything of the kind had been done, to adopt the principle in the Government offices, and in all suitable occupations, of the substitution of women's labour for men's. We pressed this on the Government with the double motive—to increase the demand for women's labour, and to set free a large number of men of military age who were keenly anxious to join the newly forming armies Our suggestion met with no response. But I cannot but look back with gratification that we made it at that early date.

While out-of-work distress lasted among women, we opened, in various parts of the country, forty workshops, and gave employment to over 2,000 women. I well remember the resentment and melancholy of some able young women in our employment when they saw the advertisements everywhere displayed calling upon young men to join the colours, announcing in huge letters YOUR COUNTRY WANTS YOU, and reflected that their country did not want them. We endeavoured, so far as lay in our power, to check this feeling of discontent by not diminishing our own demand for the services of women. We did not add to the volume of unemployment by dismissing on account of the war any of our staff or organizers. We paid the salaries and lent the services of nearly 150 trained workers all over the country to local relief committees and other bodies responsible for carrying out new work connected with the war.

The officers of our societies in many parts of the country showed great initiative in finding out what the soldiers wanted, and doing it for them. As an example, I may mention the case of the hon. secretary of one of our Kentish societies. It was in the neighbourhood of a large training camp where 12,000 men were congregated. The existing local arrangements for their laundry were quite inadequate, and this lady, of University education, ran a laundry for them most successfully and efficiently. She appealed not only to the well-to-do, but also to domestic servants and other working women in the neighbourhood, to give time regularly in their afternoons to do the necessary mending. She herself devoted her whole time to the work of the laundry, which was a great success from the first.

The London society of the N.U.W.S.S. devoted its great powers and wide experience of London conditions to sorting out efficient women workers to positions where such services, paid or unpaid, were urgently required. This work, under the name of Women's Service, it has continued, with success and efficiency, to the present time. Its energies have been remarkably varied. For instance, it provided the London General Omnibus Company with a hundred women conductors when first the need for them was felt; it was constantly applied to by the War Office and other public departments for women fitted to carry out all kinds of novel employments, such as the judging of the quality and the forwarding of hay for the army. It registered the first great rush of the Belgian refugees, and organized this so efficiently that, when the numbers to be dealt with became so great that the work had to be handed over to Government officials, no change in the system of registration had to be introduced. The London society has from the beginning of the war greatly extended the area of women's employment. It opened a small workshop and taught women acetylene welding for aeroplane work until this establishment was taken over by the Government. H.M. the Queen honoured this workshop by a surprise visit in the summer of 1916, and pleased the workers very much by taking a workshop cup of tea seated on an overturned packing-case.

I believe all our societies, from Cornwall to Stornoway, except those in the prohibited areas, did their part in providing hospitality for the Belgian refugees. The London society opened nine hostels for them in its area, and forwarded to the Government several hundred offers of private hospitality.

Over sixty of our societies, immediately after the declaration of war, devoted themselves to life-saving activities by the formation of maternity centres, baby clinics, schools for mothers, and other similar associations.

Forty-five of our societies became Red Cross centres. One of our societies, within a very few weeks of the outbreak of war, offered to staff and equip a hospital at a naval base in the North of Scotland, but the chief medical officer and the C.O. rejected the offer, with the remark that they did not wish to be troubled by " hysterical women." The officers and members of our societies were extremely active in establishing and providing the necessary funds and labour for keeping up canteens for soldiers on railway-stations, also in starting clubs, guest-rooms, and houses of rest for soldiers. At many of these educational facilities were given, French classes being particularly called for. We also did everything in our power to call attention to and to check the terrible waste which at the outset was taking place in the training camps for soldiers; and our organization was first in the field, afterwards so well tilled by the war savings committees, to call attention to the great national importance of personal and household economy. Many of our most active societies initiated war savings exhibitions and demonstrations in their own area, and by precept and practice showed the great national importance of personal thrift. In London, Liverpool, Cardiff, Brighton, and many other places, we held these

" patriotic housekeeping " exhibitions, where short
addresses were given, war economy recipes dis-
tributed, etc.   To women of all classes who constantly passed through them we did not fail to
bring home the importance of small daily savings,
showing that if every one of us in our domestic
expenditure could save on an average twopence a
head per day, Sundays excepted, this would be a
shilling a week, and a shilling a week for 45,000,000
people, fifty-two weeks in the year, meant an
annual saving of £117,000,000.   In this way we
countered the so-called " argument " so frequently
heard: " What is the good of my saving my poor
little pence when the Government is throwing away
millions in absolute waste, for which no one is a
farthing the better ?"   Women, we reminded our
audiences, everywhere and in all classes, were the
domestic Chancellors of the Exchequer: domestic
expenditure was almost wholly in their hands.
Women had often been told in contempt that their
business was to " mind the kitchen "; and now they
joyfully and proudly determined they would mind
the kitchen, and do their part in the service of their
country by saving hundreds of millions per year;
and they also determined to do this while seeing that
by skilful management the physical health of those
under their charge was in no way impaired.   Their
job was to see that every ounce of raw material passing through their hands yielded its full food value.

I have already touched in an earlier chapter on the most important of all the war activities of the N.U.W.S.S.—the Scottish Women's Hospitals for Foreign Service, initiated and carried through by the genius and devotion of the hon. secretary of our Scottish Federation, Dr. Elsie Inglis. Her name and her great work are now known and honoured throughout the world, and it is unnecessary here to dwell upon them at any length. In the old days before the war Dr. Inglis used to say she had two passions, " suffrage and surgery." Before the end of her honoured life came she added to these two S's yet another, " Serbia." How this came about is worth recalling, and can be studied in detail in the " Life of Dr. Elsie Inglis, " by Lady Frances Balfour. It affords an example of " the soul of goodness in things evil would men observingly distil it out." Her first wish in September, 1914, was to place her services, her knowledge and skill in her profession, at the service of her country. In an interview with a high official of the R.A.M.C. at the War Office in that month, when she asked his advice as to what course she should take, his reply was: " Dear lady, go home and keep quiet "—in other words, her help was refused. The British Red Cross adopted the same attitude. She was therefore compelled to place her organization under the French Red Cross. The great hospital at Royaumont was the first to be established. The N.U.W.S.S. Scottish Women's

Hospitals were complete hospital units, officered entirely by women. The physicians and surgeons, nurses, dressers, orderlies, motor drivers, and domestic staff were all women. The whole scheme was initiated by Dr. Elsie Inglis, and was enthusiastically taken up by the whole N.U.W.S.S. The work quickly grew to large proportions. I have a letter from Dr. Inglis, dated October 13th, 1914, on the financial aspect of her scheme. At that date she only had £213 in hand. At the date of writing this, August 18th, 1919, the total collected for the S.W.H. amounted to £428,905 1s. 3d. The total number of beds in France and Serbia for which the organization was responsible exceeded 1,800. Powerful committees were formed in Scotland, South Wales, and in London to support the hospitals, and their membership was not confined to the N.U.W.S.S.—indeed, especially in Scotland, several influential non-suffragists joined in promoting the great work. It must not for a moment be supposed that only suffragists were active and devoted. It was recognized by the instinctive common sense of the great majority of women throughout the whole country, suffragist and non-suffragist, militant and non-militant, that their first duty was by every practical means in their power to strengthen the resources of their country so as to aid it to issue successfully from the great struggle. Those who took a contrary view did exist, but their numbers were very small. But it is a source of pride and thankfulness that the womanhood of the whole country, quite irrespective of political party or creed, were eager to do everything in their power to help their country. The " militants " immediately abandoned militant tactics. Many of them took part in what was known as the Women's Emergency Corps, which readily undertook a large variety of patriotic activities. Several well-known antisuffragists, among them Mrs. Humphry Ward and Miss Gladys Pott, did patriotic work of a first-class kind. Among the former " militants," two, Dr. Flora Murray and Dr. Louisa Garrett Anderson, were, I believe, the very first women doctors to take out a well-equipped hospital unit, officered entirely by women, to France. The necessary funds were privately subscribed. It was of these ladies that Surgeon-General Sir Alfred Keogh, head of the R.A.M.C., afterwards said that they " were worth their weight, not in gold, but in diamonds." He had by this time had practical experience of their professional and personal work, both in Paris and, later, in another hospital at Wimereux. Sir Alfred Keogh's words were no empty compliment, for he very shortly afterwards placed Dr. F. Murray and Dr. L. G. Anderson at the head of a large military hospital of 520 beds in London, posts which carried the rank of Major in the army.

Their first hospital was established in a spacious

7

hotel in the Champs Elysées, and was described as the best equipped in Paris. It became quite a show place, and those who visited it were full of admiration for the devotion, care, and skill with which the patients were tended. The men were most grateful and appreciative of the skill of the women surgeons, dressers, and nurses. " There was a wonderful atmosphere of sympathy and home about the wards, and the men were not slow to respond to it," wrote a visitor. Another visitor asked one of the wounded men: " Is it possible there are no men surgeons in this place ?" The man, a Highlander, replied by another question: " And what would we be wanting men for ?" Other hospitals officered by women were taken out to Belgium and the North of France quite independently of the N.U.W.S.S.; but the Scottish Women's Hospitals were the only ones which were originated and run, as one of their main pieces of war work, by a suffrage organization.

Our first unit arrived at the Abbaye de Royaumont in December, 1914. The building had then been uninhabited for about ten years, and was a bare shell, without water, light, or heating; magnificent indeed architecturally, but almost incredibly forbidding, icy cold, dark, and comfortless.

The forerunners will not easily forget the first few weeks in the Abbaye, when they had to cope with the difficulties of converting this dark ice-house into warm and comfortable wards for sick and wounded soldiers. But it was done cheerfully, and even gaily. Outside labour was practically impossible to get, and the whole staff turned to and did the work themselves: charing and scrubbing went on; electric light and electric stoves were procured; the equipment arrived; the pioneers after a time had the pleasure of sleeping in beds instead of on the floors, and by the middle of January, 1915, the huge vaulted halls were all white and spotless, and were transformed into comfortable wards, with rows of cosy beds covered with cheery red blankets. There were 100 beds to begin with, but this number quickly grew to 200; then to 400; and eventually, in the very last months of the war, to 600.

The Medical Department of the French Army, probably a little sceptical at first, visited the hospital, examined it thoroughly, and expressed their warm approval, especially of the X-ray apparatus which was the only one for many miles round, and of the very practical character of the whole equipment.

Gradually the most difficult and serious cases among French soldiers gravitated to this hospital. General Joffre showed a very kindly interest in it, and on one occasion sent an aide-de-camp with a gift of money for distribution among the patients as they left. The medical and surgical work done has been of the very highest excellence, and was warmly appreciated by the patients. The women surgeons made a great study of conservative surgery, and many a wounded man left Royaumont with limbs intact, saved by the skill and patience of the Scottish Women's unit.

The second hospital to be opened in France was at Troyes. It was financed by the students of Newnham and Girton, a fact which is said to have made a deep impression on the French soldiers. This hospital was directly under the French military authorities, and when the complications in the Balkans became acute it was ordered to Salonica. An enlargement of this hospital, financed by our Manchester society, was under the medical direction of Dr. Mary Blair. When Serbia was overrun by the Austrians her unit was transferred to Corsica, where she had control of a hospital for Serbian refugees at Ajaccio.

The N.U.W.S.S. eventually had five units in Serbia. One of the most magnificent pieces of work they did was the successful grappling, under Dr. Inglis's guidance, with the typhus epidemic in 1915, which threatened the very existence of the Serbian Army. It may be said that twice Dr. Inglis saved the Serbian nation from despair—once when she stamped out the typhus epidemic, and once when the country was overrun by the then victorious Germans and Austrians. This compelled the withdrawal of most of our units. The papers told of their wonderful tramp of 300 miles across ice-bound mountains. Dr. Elsie Inglis and Dr. Alice Hutchinson, with their respective staffs, did not leave Serbia when the other units left. They stayed on and continued their work until they were taken prisoners by the Austrians. They were prisoners for three months. Dr. Alice Hutchinson told how she and her unit kept Christmas, 1915:

" In the evening we sang carols and drank toasts. We even ventured to sing ' God save the King ' under our breath. . . . It cheered us wonderfully. We had our British flag with us, too. I wound it round my body under my clothes when we evacuated our hospital, so that it should not be trampled on and insulted " (*The Common Cause*, February 18th, 1916).

She refused to give up her hospital equipment without a receipt, and on being ordered to send her unit to a cholera hospital, she refused, except on condition that her nurses were first inoculated, and also paid for their work, and their proper rank accorded to the doctors. " At this," she said, " there was a terrible scene. I was sworn at and cursed, and told I was a coward; but I would not give in." She was willing to work herself for cholera patients, but would not allow her nurses to do so without inoculation.

Dr. Elsie Inglis also showed the same fine spirit. They both said that the Germans, officers and men alike, behaved like brutes, the latter using disgusting and insulting language. The Austrians, officers and men, were kind and polite. But the hardships of the imprisonment were shortage of food and gross overcrowding. Our doctors were enthusiastic in all they said of the courage and devotion of the Serbians. They reached home safe and sound, and made an appeal for additional subscriptions to continue their splendid work.

The scientific work done by the women doctors at Royaumont received an unsolicited testimonial in 1916 from a leading French man of science, Dr. Weinberg, who held the office of Chef de Laboratoire at the Pasteur Institute, Paris.

Lecturing to members of the medical profession in Glasgow on gas gangrene, he paid a splendid tribute to the work of the Scottish Women's Hospital at Royaumont. He had, he said, seen hundreds and hundreds of military hospitals, but none the organization and direction of which won his admiration so completely. Every duty in the hospital, from those of the chief surgeon to the chauffeur of the motor ambulance, was performed by women. He was impelled to express his admiration of the manner in which cases were treated. The military authorities had such confidence in the hospital that they were ready to trust to its care the most severe class of cases. Of the bacteriological department of the hospital, which was arranged by Dr. Elizabeth Butler, Dr. Weinberg was equally enthusiastic. He was struck with the most perfect order which prevailed, notwithstanding the apparent entire absence of anything in the form of rigid disciplinary measures. He attributed this order to the fact that the patients recognized how devoted were the staff to their care and interests. It was the soldier's natural recognition of the excellent services and attention given by all the staff, and particularly by the chief surgeon, Miss Ivens, who was ably assisted by numerous colleagues all inspired by the same devotion. Incidentally, Dr. Weinberg expressed the opinion that he could not imagine any activity on the part of women that would more effectively further the cause of the women's movement than the institutions carried on by the Scottish Women's Hospitals.

The work of the hospital at Royaumont was particularly heavy in the spring of 1918. The place was frequently exposed to bombardment. The three operating theatres were kept busy night and day, the surgeons having frequently to work by candlelight and under shell-fire. In July the hospital was taken over by the French military authorities, when the number of beds was brought up to 600. Down to the very end of the war the work of the Scottish Women's Hospitals was continued in France and Serbia undiminished in vigour and extent. In October and November, 1918, the organization was maintaining 1,885 beds. Many of the doctors and nurses have received decorations and other honours from the French and Serbian nations; but, so far as I know, no national honour has been conferred on them by the country of their birth. In recognition of her splendid work, the chief medical officer at Royaumont, Dr. Frances Ivens, received the Croix de Guerre avec Palme, and twenty-three of her staff the Croix de Guerre avec Etoiles from the French Army. In February, 1919, the hospital was closed; but the organization of the Scottish Women's Hospitals still exists. The committee at headquarters in Edinburgh are raising a fund to establish a training school for Serbian nurses in Belgrade as a memorial to Dr. Elsie Inglis; while the London committee, with the same object in view, are in process of endowing a chair of medicine in the University of Belgrade. The name of Elsie Inglis will live for ever in Serbian history. Her works do follow her, and her memory will be cherished by the gallant nation to which she devoted her great powers.

Late in the autumn of 1915 the N.U.W.S.S. resolved to send some units of women doctors and nurses to Russia to aid the civil population, more especially women and children, who had become refugees in consequence of the German advance over the western provinces of Russia. The accounts which reached us of the sufferings of these refugees were terrible. The roads by which they had travelled were marked by the graves of those who had fallen by the wayside. A maternity hospital was opened in Petrograd as well as "barak" hospitals for all kinds of infectious diseases. Our units were warmly welcomed by the suffering population and by the Zemstvos. They co-operated with the Britain to Poland Fund Committee, and also with the Moscow Union of Zemstvos. Eight hospitals were equipped and opened. Our doctors and their staffs on their arrival immediately began a fierce fight with diphtheria, scarlet fever, smallpox, typhus, and scabies; and skilled treatment saved many hundreds of lives. Over £11,000 was raised, and we were served by most able and devoted staffs, several of whom laid down their lives in the work in which they had engaged. The work was brought to a premature end by the chaos which quickly supervened upon the Russian Revolution of March, 1917. The N.U.W.S.S. did me the honour of naming the Russian units after me. The doctors and nurses of the M.F. Hospitals returned finally to England in August, 1917. The welcome our units received from the Zemstvos and the students, male and female, of the University of Kazan made us feel that they were appreciated, and we can only trust that, like other good seed, the work of our units will bring forth fruit in due season.

CHAPTER VIII

WOMEN'S WAR WORK AS IT AFFECTED PUBLIC OPINION

" A land of settled Government,
A land of just and old renown,
Where Freedom slowly broadens down
From precedent to precedent."

THE war revolutionized the industrial position of women. It found them serfs and left them free. It not only opened to them opportunities of employment in a number of skilled trades, but, more important even than this, it revolutionized men's minds and their conception of the sort of work of which the ordinary everyday woman was capable. It opened men's eyes to the national waste involved in condemning women to forms of work needing only very mediocre intelligence. It also opened their eyes to the national as well as the personal value of the ordinary domestic work of women, which has been in their hands for uncounted generations. It ploughed up the hardened soil of ancient prejudice, dissolving it and replacing it by a soil capable of fructifying the seeds of new ideas. Not even the most inveterate of antisuffragists could have ventured to say, after the experience gained by the war, what one of them quoted on a previous page had said just before the war, to the effect that, apart from breeding, women were of no national importance whatever.

It made women themselves, as well as men, realize the great national importance of women's ordinary domestic work. One example which went the round of the Press will illustrate this. In a convalescent camp of 2,820 men in the South of England the employment of women cooks in the place of men caused a saving in one month of £900, and at the same time the men were better and not worse fed. The saving was not effected by cutting down the wages bill or by stinting the supplies, but by the more skilful use of food-stuffs and the sensible expedient of employing those who knew their job in the place of those who did not. As an example, it may be mentioned that in many soldiers' camps, employing men cooks, the tea, served out in ample quantities and of excellent quality, was thrown away in consequence of the adoption of the odious and filthy trick of boiling the water for it in the same vessels, uncleansed, in which the meat for the mid-day dinner had been boiled. The result was illustrative of bad work in general; the tea was wasted, the men were disgruntled, and a general impression created that Government property could be thrown away without doing any harm to anyone.

John Bright used to say that the one good thing

about war was that it taught people geography. If he were living now he might very truly say that it taught people political economy; that a nation grows rich by producing, and not by destroying; that all waste is creative of poverty. War even illuminates the abstruse and difficult subject of foreign exchanges, and shows that no nation grows rich by printing promises to pay on pieces of paper. War also teaches the supreme national value of life, and illuminates Ruskin's saying, "There is no wealth but life." It is a realization of this which has fundamentally raised the position of women in every country which has come within the radius of its great searchlights.

The actual steps by which the war raised the industrial status of women from serfdom to freedom are not difficult to trace. In the first eighteen months of the war more than five million young men from every class, but mainly from the flower of the industrial population, volunteered for military service. Before the end of the war Great Britain was maintaining in the war more than eight and a half million men.* This naturally left a shortage of labour in nearly all industries, including agriculture. Naturally also there was, simultaneously with this reduction in numbers of the men in industry, a huge

* Of these 8,654,467, more than 7,000,000 were white men enlisted within the British Empire. (See Report of War Cabinet published in August, 1919.)

increase in the demand of our own Government and the Governments of our Allies for arms and ammunition, cloth for uniforms, boots, ships, hutments, food for the armies, optical glass, and every sort of military equipment. Every man and woman who could work in the fields or factories producing these things could get continuous employment at wages higher than had ever before been paid. In September, 1915, after fourteen months of war, the rate of unemployment registered at Labour Exchanges was only ½ per cent., the lowest on record. The weekly sum paid in wages had gone up by the end of October by £519,484. In March of the same year what is known as the Treasury agreement with the Trade Unionists came into existence, by which the trade unions consented, in face of the national emergency, to suspend for the duration of the war their rules and customs which prevented the employment of women in most of the skilled trades. The Treasury, on its part, gave a solemn promise not to use women as a reservoir of cheap labour, and agreed to give the same wages for the same output, and, moreover, to restore by Act of Parliament when the war was over the pre-war practices of trade unions, which had severely limited the employment of women. Women themselves were not in any way consulted when this agreement was arrived at. They were, therefore, not parties to it; and suffragists generally, while welcoming the breaking down of the barriers which prevented women having a free choice in industry, even if this were only temporary, felt that the restoration of pre-war practices by Act of Parliament when the war was concluded would make the industrial position of women, in a sense, worse than ever; for formerly, as they pointed out, women were excluded from nearly all the best paid trades simply by the rules of private societies: it was a different and a worse position to be excluded from them by statute.

In 1915, however, it was from every point of view of the first importance to get the trade union embargo on women's labour removed; and when it was removed, instantly evidence began to pour in of the high productivity of women's work. It was almost ridiculous to watch the amazement of the ordinary man when he saw how rapidly women learned men's jobs, and how, by their patriotic zeal and entire innocence of the trade union practice of ca' canny, their output frequently exceeded, and exceeded largely, the output of men working the same machinery for the same number of hours. The first evidence which reached the public of the high efficiency of women's labour was contained in an article in the trade journal *The Engineer* of August 20th, 1915, the following passage from which is here quoted:

"There is a widespread idea that the only machines which women can work are automatic or semiautomatic tools with which it is impossible to make mistakes. This idea is being daily disproved in the factory to which we have referred above, where some most delicate operations, necessitating the exercise of great skill and high intelligence, are being performed. We need only mention one case, but it will appeal to every mechanical engineer. In a certain screwing operation it was customary before the employment of women to rough the thread out with the tool, and then to finish it off with taps. Some trouble having arisen owing to the wearing of the taps, the women of their own initiative did away with the second operation, and are now accurately chasing out the threads to gauge with the tool alone. This is work of which any mechanic might feel proud. . . . In fact, it may be stated with absolute truth that women have shown themselves perfectly capable of performing operations which have hitherto been exclusively carried out by men."

Sir William Beardmore, then President of the Iron and Steel Institute, and Chairman of the Park-head Ironworks, Glasgow, spoke in his presidential address of the high productivity of women's labour. He quoted the case of a new machine introduced by his firm, of which it was desired to test the utility. A good workman was induced with some difficulty to try it and to lay aside, for the sake of the experiment, the traditional restriction of output. The machine did well, but not so well as the firm had been led to expect. Then another experiment was made, that of putting women on the job. " Using the same machines, and working the same number of hours, their output was more than double that of the thoroughly trained mechanic." The newspapers about this time began to be full of articles praising up to the skies the "wonderful," "amazing," "extraordinary" mechanical capability of women. The case was quoted of a woman, formerly a charwoman, who had been put on to do gun breech work. Her job was to bore a hole $\frac{1}{8}$ inch in diameter dead true through 12 inches of solid steel. The test was the tally of broken tools, and at the time of writing this woman, the former "char," had a clean slate. Every successive Minister of Munitions, and almost every other Minister, spoke enthusiastically of the extraordinary value to the nation of women's work. Mr. Lloyd George said: "Their work is absolutely indispensable, and they themselves are extraordinarily adaptable." And again: "I am anxious to bear testimony to the tremendous part played by the women of England in this vital epoch of human history." Mr. Montagu said in the House of Commons in his first speech after becoming Minister of Munitions: "Women of every station, with or without previous experience . . have proved themselves able to undertake work which before the war was regarded solely as the province of men, and often of skilled men alone. Indeed, it is not too much to say that our armies have been saved and victory assured by the women in the munition factories." Mr. Churchill confessed that without the work of women it would have been im-

PRO PATRIA : A TRIBUTE TO WOMAN'S WORK IN WAR-TIME.

(Reproduced by special permission of the Proprietors of *Punch*.)

Punch, January 26, 1916.]

[Facing page 112.

possible to win the war; and also referred to the excellence of its quality, as well as the enormous character of its volume.

Lord Selborne, as Minister of Agriculture, gave unstinted praise to women's work on farms, and said he had heard nothing but unqualified praise of the hundreds of women thus employed.

All the foregoing we were able to reckon among the supporters of women's political enfranchisement. But we began to be aware of a new note among the voices that go to make up public opinion when we discovered commercial and financial magnates, managers of railways and other great industrial concerns, and old-fashioned country gentlemen not hitherto connected in any way with our political aims, joining in the chorus which was now loudly chanting the praises of women's work.

A very interesting and important article on Women in Industry will be found in the *Quarterly Review*, July, 1919, by Sir Lynden Macassey, Chairman of the National Tribunal on Women's Wages, Chairman of the Clyde Dilution Commission, and a member of the War Cabinet Committee on Women in Industry. In this *Quarterly* article, among other significant things, he says that by the end of the war "women had literally leapt as agents of production, and by inherent economic powers and aptitude, into a position of eminence in the economic world previously undreamt of even by themselves" (p. 79).

8

On another page he says that, "where the work required constant alertness, a sure, deft touch, delicacy of manipulation—in short, a combination of quick intelligence and manual dexterity within a limited ambit—women were invariably superior to men "(p. 81). I, for one, can never believe that any Act of Parliament can thrust women back into the industrial morass in which they were stifled before the war.

Lord Revelstoke, speaking as an expert on finance, said that the tapping of the "new reservoir" of women's labour had saved the financial situation by enabling the country to keep up the volume of its exports. Even Lord Curzon, Chairman of the Antisuffrage League, and Mr. Asquith, our chief political adversary, surprised us by joining with Mr. Balfour in signing a letter to the Press containing a strong appeal for funds for the extension of the buildings of the London School of Medicine for Women. "Is Saul also among the prophets?" we asked each other. Mr. Walter Long, at that date an opponent of our enfranchisement, included women in his National Register Bill, saying that women themselves had made an almost unanimous demand for this, and he would look upon their exclusion "as a serious rebuff wholly unjustifiable in face of the splendid services which they had rendered already to the prosecution of the war." Mr. Walter Long, too, had greatly delighted us at a

meeting in Grosvenor House to promote the employment of women on the land by exclaiming that,
although the movement was going on well, "yet
there were still, unfortunately, villages to be found
where the women had become imbued with the idea
that woman's place is home." "That idea," he
added, "must be met and combated."

Even more extraordinary, however, were the signs
which now began to be seen of Mr. Asquith's change
of view. This was first foreshadowed in his words
spoken in the House of Commons on the heroic
death of Edith Cavell in September, 1915. Referring to what that year had produced to justify
"faith in the manhood and womanhood of our
people," he added, speaking particularly of Miss
Cavell: "She has taught the bravest man amongst
us a supreme lesson of courage; yes, and in this
United Kingdom and throughout the Dominions
of the Crown there are thousands of such women,
but a year ago we did not know it." We suffragists
rejoiced in this change of tone. At the same time,
we wondered where he could have lived all his sixty
odd years without discovering that courage was not
the exclusive attribute of the male sex. At this
time—1916, 1917—conversions of important public
men and of newspapers came in, not by twos and
threes, but by battalions. The Press became full
of wonderful instances of women's courage and
capacity, and told of nurses standing back from the

lifeboats of a torpedoed ship, who, when the word
went forth, " Save the women first," gave the reply,
" Fighting men first; they are the country's greatest
need." The Prefect of Constanza was quoted,
who saw the work of our women orderlies in connection with the Scottish Women's Hospitals, and said:
" It is extraordinary how these women endure hardships; they refuse help, and carry the wounded
themselves. They work like navvies. No wonder
England is a great country if the women are like
that." Another instance of the courage of women
which deeply affected public opinion was afforded
at an inquest on the bodies of the victims of an
explosion at a shell factory in the North of England.
Twenty-six women had been killed, and about thirty
injured. The behaviour of the women was declared
to be worthy of the highest praise. " They displayed the greatest coolness and perfect discipline,
both in helping to remove the injured and in con-
tinuing to carry on the work of the factory." It
was announced in the Press that Sir Douglas Haig
would be asked to let the men at the front know
of the courage and spirit which animated their
womenfolk at home. Our feeling about all this was,
not that women had changed, but that the public
attitude towards them and appreciation of them had
changed.

Among the conversions to suffrage views at
this time, none were more valuable to us than

Man of the World (lighting up): "We'll 'ave to give it 'em, I expect, Chorlie!"

(Reproduced by special permission of the Proprietors of *Punch*.)

Punch, November 30, 1910]

[Facing page 116.

those of which we had evidence in the Press. Our old friends the *Manchester Guardian*, the *Daily News*, the *Aberdeen Free Press*, the *Nation*, the *New Statesman*, etc., stood by us, and were more valued than ever; but we welcomed new recruits in *The Times*, the *Daily Mail*, the *Globe*, the *Evening News*, and *Observer*. Miss Violet Markham, once a chief among the antisuffragists, was known to have withdrawn her opposition. Her war work had brought her in contact with some of our most active societies, and she was understood to have said that she would never in future say anything against suffragists. Her conversion may be assumed to have been fairly complete, as she consented to stand as a Liberal candidate for the Mansfield Division of Nottinghamshire at the General Election in December, 1918. One of our chief opponents in the Press was reported to have said: " The women were wonderful ! Their adaptability, freshness of mind, and organizing skill were magnificent. Men were making too great a mess of the world, and needed helpers without their own prejudices, idleness, and self-indulgence."

The conversion of other well-known public men, formerly our opponents, became known about this time. Among these may be mentioned Lord Derby and his brother, Sir Arthur Stanley, Chairman of the British Red Cross and St. John of Jerusalem Nursing Association; Lord Faber, Mr. Winston Churchill, Sir Arthur Conan Doyle, and Sir Croydon

Marks. Two former antisuffragists, both Members of Parliament, one a Liberal and the other a Conservative, may be quoted as representative of what was going on in men's minds. The Liberal, who had hitherto pleaded militancy as an excuse for his antisuffragism, said at the annual meeting of Liberals in his constituency: "Any party which did not realize that the women had made good their cause by their services where they had formerly spoilt it by their threats must be blind"; and he held there should be no widening of the franchise for men without bringing in women on the same terms. The Conservative said simply: "I have always been an antisuffragist, but the women have served their country so magnificently that after this I shall support giving them the vote."

It is very significant that, while these wholesale conversions were taking place in this country, thus preparing the way for a sweeping victory for women's suffrage in the House of Commons, a similar change, brought about by similar causes, had already, in 1916, taken place in Canada. In that year a great suffrage movement swept over Canada, like a mighty wind, from the West to the East. One after another, Alberta, Saskatchewan, Manitoba, and British Columbia enfranchised their women. In British Columbia, a referendum (only men voting) showed a majority of more than two to one for women's franchise, and the soldiers' vote, which came in later, only swelled the large majority. Ontario followed. The late Sir Wilfred Laurier, once Liberal Premier, announced his conversion. He had for years been an important opponent.

The Nova Scotia legislature passed a Women's Suffrage Bill without opposition; and in May, 1917, Sir Robert Borden announced his intention to introduce a women's suffrage measure for the whole of Canada, thus giving women the federal vote. This intention was faithfully carried into effect in time for women to vote at the General Election, which was held in 1917. The Province of Alberta, in the meantime, had bettered its own record by returning a lady, Miss Roberta Catherine MacAdams, to its Legislative Assembly. An interesting feature of her election was that she was chosen entirely by men who were performing military service in Europe. There were twenty men candidates and one woman, and Miss MacAdams was elected. Thus the whole Empire seemed by one impulse to be moving in the direction of women's enfranchisement.

About this time a professional man of wide outlook and long experience wrote:

" One of the greatest benefits which I look for from the war is that women will come by their own. The tribute to the efficiency of women's work now being paid by managers of railways and munition works—many of them unwilling witnesses—are most hopeful signs. After this it seems impossible that women should be

denied their fair share in the national councils.
This opens a wide vista of other resulting reforms,
which almost makes one wish to be young again,
so that one might see what will happen in the next
fifty years."

Women did come by their own, not quite
directly, but through "the verdurous gloom and
winding mossy ways" of the parliamentary wrangle
over the Special Register Bill and the Speaker's
conference to be described in the next chapter.

CHAPTER IX

THE LAST PHASE

" It eonsists of an influx—whence or why none can tell—
of a wave of vitality. It is as if from the central heart of
life a ray broke suddenly upon the world, inspiring men
to feel deeply, to live greatly, to do nobly. It makes men.
It is not made by men."

WITHOUT belittling the importance of the wave of
enthusiasm for women's enfranchisement which
swept over the English-speaking world in 1916,
it is impossible to disguise the fact that we in
England won our battle at the exact moment we
did in consequence of the absolute necessity under
which the Government laboured of producing a new
parliamentary register and a new voting qualification for men. For this meant that a real reform
of the representation of the people was required; and
the previous stages of our political struggle had
demonstrated that when once the franchise question
was dealt with by Parliament it would be impossible
any longer to neglect the claims of women.

It will be remembered that so long ago as 1892
Mr. A. J. Balfour had said in a suffrage debate in
Parliament:

" If any further alteration of the franchise is brought forward as a practical measure, this question [the enfranchisement of women] will again arise, menacing and ripe for solution, and it will not be possible for this House to set it aside as a mere speculative plan advocated by a group of faddists. Then you will have to deal with the problem of women's suffrage, and deal with it in a complete fashion."

The moment which Mr. Balfour foresaw in 1892 had arrived in 1916. The situation was briefly thus : The old register for the whole United Kingdom, unrevised by the express direction of the Government since the outbreak of the world war, contained the names of rather over eight million men, of whom almost seven millions voted as " occupiers " or householders. There were other qualifications, such as the lodger, freehold, and University franchises; but they only accounted, between them, for about a million voters in the three kingdoms. " Occupation " was, therefore, by far the most important of the qualifications for the exercise of the parliamentary franchise. To qualify as an " occupier " it was, however, necessary to prove the unbroken occupation of the qualifying premises for twelve months previous to the last 15th of July. This obviously necessitated in some cases continuous residence for nearly two years. From August, 1914, onwards at least five millions of men, either actual or potential voters, had volunteered for the Navy or Army, or had moved, in obedience to national demands, to munition areas, or other places where they were required. Consequently very large numbers had ceased to be " occupiers " in the sense legally required to enable them to become, or remain, voters.

The Government and the country were therefore, in the third year of the war, face to face with the impossible position that if circumstances necessitated an appeal to the country there was in existence no register of voters which could in any sense be looked upon as representative of the manhood of the nation. The elderly, the infirm, the shirker, the crank, who had remained at home evading military service, and " the conscientious objector," would remain on the old and obsolete register in full numerical strength; the young manhood of the nation who were fighting for it in the Navy, or the Air Service, or on the dreary swamps of Flanders, or the tremendous battlefields round Ypres or on the Somme, would in large proportion have forfeited their parliamentary votes in consequence of the services they were rendering to their country. It was an intolerable situation. By-elections which from time to time took place illustrated the extraordinarily non-representative character of the old register. Candidates and agents reported the existence of street after street in which only a handful of voters remained. It would have been impossible to dissolve on such a register, and even if it had been possible, Mr. Asquith had himself declared that a Parliament elected on such a register would be " lacking in moral sanction."

It will be remembered that the House elected in 1910 had passed an Act limiting the duration of all future Parliaments to five years. If there had been no war the dissolution must therefore have taken place by 1915; but as a General Election, except on sheer necessity, could not be contemplated during the war, the operation of the five years' limit was more than once suspended by legislation. This, however, was only postponing the problem, and did not afford any solution of it.

Mr. Asquith's first War Cabinet had suddenly collapsed in May, 1915, and had been succeeded by the first Coalition Government. Mr. Asquith remained Prime Minister, but among his colleagues were now found representatives of the three chief parties—Liberal, Conservative, and Labour. Mr. Redmond, as leader of the Irish Nationalists, was also asked to join it, but declined to do so. The changes involved in this reconstitution of the Government were in several ways favourable to the suffrage movement: not a few of our most bigoted opponents were among the Liberals who were shed by Mr. Asquith when he formed his Coalition Government, whilst among his new colleagues were now to be found convinced suffragists, such as Mr. A. J. Balfour, Mr. Bonar Law, Lord Robert Cecil, Lord

Lytton, Lord Selborne, Mr. Arthur Henderson, etc.
The formation of the coalition was favourable to
us in another sense. Party discipline and party
passion had always been inimical to our movement.
" Yes, I am your friend, but I am not prepared to
break up my party in order to support you," said
one party leader. " Yes, I am your friend, but I
tell you frankly, you must not count on my vote if
the success of women's suffrage would mean the
withdrawal from public life of my leader, Mr.
Asquith," said another. I had been accustomed
to say of the two chief parties, Liberal and Conservative, that from the suffrage point of view the
first was an army without generals, and the second
was generals without an army. The Coalition gave
us the immense advantage of bringing these two
indispensable elements of success together, and
parliamentary suffragists became equally strong
in both officers and men. The commander-in-chief,
Mr. Asquith, was still our opponent, but, as described
in the last chapter, we began to see signs that even
he was prepared to recognize that he was beaten,
and to ask for an armistice.

When 1916 arrived no solution of the franchise
problem had been found; the creation of a new
register before a General Election could be held
was generally recognized as necessary, but there
were no signs of agreement upon the principles on
which it should be based. The end of the war

seemed as far off as ever. Compulsory military service for men had been adopted, and this strengthened the demand for manhood suffrage on the very reasonable ground that if a man could be compelled to offer his life for his country, he should at least have some influence, as a voter, in controlling the policy which might cause such a sacrifice to be called for.

Contemporaneously with these events and new developments, Sir Edward Carson and a group of his parliamentary supporters were urging with considerable vigour that there should be a new franchise based on military service. In a sense he had a strong position, for it was an obvious absurdity that men offering their lives for their country should incidentally to the fulfilment of that service be struck off the parliamentary register, while every waster and do-nothing who managed to stay at home maintaining his occupation franchise would have the vote. We made some unsuccessful efforts to induce Sir Edward Carson so to define his definition of " service " as to include the services of women. Meanwhile, there was a great deal of discussion socially and in the Press about the possibility of basing the vote on national service of some kind.

On May 4th, 1916, we addressed a careful letter to Mr. Asquith on the points raised by the obsolete register and the necessity for a new one, and also for a new qualification for the franchise. We said that nothing was farther from our intention than to press our claim at such a moment if the Government was contemplating legislation simply to replace on the register those men who had lost their qualification in consequence of their service in the Navy or Army, or in munition areas in parts of the country other than those where they had formerly resided. But we stated that if the Government intended to meet the situation by altering the whole basis of the parliamentary franchise and founding it on national service, whether naval, military, or industrial, we should then use our utmost endeavours to induce a favourable consideration at the same time of the national services of women. After referring to some of the very important work of women during the war, we added:

" When the Government deals with the franchise, an opportunity will present itself of dealing with it on wider lines than by the simple removal of what may be called the accidental disqualification of a large body of the best men in the country, and we trust that you may include in your Bill clauses which would remove the disabilities under which women now labour. An agreed Bill on these lines would, we are confident, receive a very wide measure of support throughout the country. Our movement has received very great accessions of strength during recent months, former opponents now declaring themselves on our side, or, at any rate, withdrawing their opposition. The change of tone in the Press is most marked. . . . The view has been widely expressed in a great variety of organs of public opinion that the continued exclusion of women from representation will . . . be an impossibility after the war."

Mr. Asquith replied almost immediately.

> " 10, DOWNING STREET,
> " WHITEHALL, S.W.,
> " *May 7th*, 1916.
>
> " DEAR MRS. FAWCETT,
> " I have received your letter of the 4th. I need not assure you how deeply my colleagues and I recognize and appreciate the magnificent contribution which the women of the United Kingdom have made to the maintenance of our country's cause.
> " No such legislation as you refer to is at present in contemplation; but if, and when, it should become necessary to undertake it, you may be certain that the considerations set out in your letter will be fully and impartially weighed without any prejudgment from the controversies of the past.
> " Yours very faithfully,
> " H. H. ASQUITH."

This reply was, we considered, very much more encouraging than any previous letter which we had received from Mr. Asquith. There were some suffragists who did not fail to point out that it promised us nothing. This we did not dispute, but we felt, all the same, that the letter indicated that the turn of the tide in the suffrage direction was taking effect, and that vessels which had long been high and dry on the sandbanks of prejudice were beginning to be floated, and would soon swing round.

On May 7th, Mr. Asquith had said in his letter, "no such legislation as you refer to is at present in contemplation." Nevertheless, it was plain two weeks later from the Prime Minister's replies to questions in the House that this attitude had already been abandoned. The Government then began a series of futile efforts to deal with the problems presented by the situation just described by means of "Special Register" Bills. None of these plans secured the support of the House of Commons. Mr. Asquith shrank from the thorough-going method of solving the problem by introducing a Reform Bill which should frankly provide a new basis for the suffrage. Such a course, he said, would bring the House "face to face with another most formidable proposition," the question of women's suffrage. Sir Edward Carson was meanwhile pressing for a new franchise giving the vote to all sailors, soldiers, and airmen, on the ground of their services. The comment of the Press on this was: "It is clear that the Bill cannot include the soldiers and exclude the women." The hesitation and reluctance of the Government to face the facts went on all through July. It was the same attitude which had caused the fiasco of the Government Bill in January, 1913 when an attempt had been made to pass a Reform Bill at the tail-end of a Session already thirteen months long by calling it a Registration Bill. On July 12th, 1916, Mr. Asquith said that the Govern-

ment, not having been able to find any practical and
non-controversial solution of the registration question, proposed that the House itself should settle
the matter.   This was not a popular method of
proceeding, but the proposition was wrapped up
with Mr. Asquith's well-known skill as a master of
parliamentary oratory; and though the House
grumbled it was not in revolt.   A week later, however, the same theme was expounded with much less
than the Prime Minister's tact by Mr. Herbert
Samuel   another well-known antisuffragist, who
enraged the House of Commons by saying in effect
the same thing as Mr. Asquith, but in a manner
which made it plain, even to the wayfaring man,
that it was because the difficulty was insoluble that
the Government requested the House of Commons
to solve it.   He set forth all the difficulties.   Something had got to be done; the old register was useless;
a new register on the old basis would be nearly as
bad, since it would disfranchise our fighting men;
and therefore the House would have to take up the
difficult controversial points of women's suffrage,
plural voting, adult suffrage, and redistribution.
The indignation of the House on being told bluntly
that the problem was handed to them to solve because it was insoluble caused it to reject the Government proposal; the matter was thrown back by the
House to the Cabinet, who were told to do their own
job; they therefore began another period of " lengthy
consideration."

In the previous spring a leading member of our
Executive Committee, Miss Rathbone, now President of the N.U.S.E.C.,* had formed a consultative committee of constitutional women's suffrage
societies, representative of twenty different organizations. This consultative committee sought and
obtained early in August an interview with Lord
Robert Cecil and Mr. Bonar Law. The deputation
urged the necessity for the enfranchisement of
women in time for them to take part in the election
of the Parliament which would have to deal with
the problems of reconstruction after the war; they
also repeated that if the new register simply replaced
on the roll of voters those men who had forfeited
their vote in consequence of their patriotic services,
we should not, during the war, raise the question
of women's suffrage at all; but if the whole basis of
the suffrage were changed we should press the consideration of women's claims with all the strength at
our command. Mr. Bonar Law expressed satisfaction
with this attitude, but asked if the suffrage societies
would stand aside if the period of residence required
of future male voters was reduced from twelve months
to three. The reply was in the negative, because
this change would in reality be equivalent to a new
suffrage, and would add many thousands of men to

* In March, 1919, the Council of the N.U.W.S.S. changed
the name of our society to the National Union of Societies
for Equal Citizenship, and elected Miss Rathbone as its
president.

the roll of voters. Lord Robert Cecil warmly supported this view, and said that the reduction in the qualifying period would constitute a long step towards manhood suffrage, and would seriously injure the position of women if nothing were done for them at the same time.

We were getting now very near the keep of the antisuffrage fortress. We heard of very prolonged and ardent discussions in the Cabinet on our question, during which the protagonists on our side were Mr. Lloyd George, Lord Robert Cecil, and Mr. Arthur Henderson, representing severally the Liberal, Conservative, and Labour Parties. Mr. Asquith and other antisuffragists clung to the position of simply replacing on the parliamentary register those men who had forfeited their vote through ceasing to be occupiers. This, however, was but rumour. What we knew as a positive fact was that the makeshift proposals brought by the Government before Parliament were rejected one after another. August 13th and 14th, 1916, were days of first-rate importance in the history of our movement. On the 13th the *Observer*, the well-known Conservative Sunday paper, up to that time a determined opponent of women's enfranchisement, contained an editorial completely and thoroughly withdrawing its opposition. Among other excellent things the editor, Mr. Garvin, wrote: " Time was when I thought that men alone maintained the

State. Now I know that men alone never could have maintained it, and that henceforth the modern State must be dependent on men and women alike for the progressive strength and vitality of its whole organization."

On the 14th Mr. Asquith, introducing yet another Special Register Bill, announced in the House of Commons a similar change of view. After acknowledging in a very handsome way the great national value of the services rendered by women to their country during the war, saying that these had been as effective as those of any other part of the population, he added:

" It is true they cannot fight in the sense of going out with rifles and so forth, but they fill our munition factories; they have aided in the most effective way in the prosecution of the war. What is more —and this is a point which makes a special appeal to me—they say, when the war comes to an end, and when these abnormal, and of course to a large extent transient, conditions have to be revised, and when the process of industrial reconstruction has to be set on foot, have not the women a special claim to be heard on the many questions which will arise directly affecting their interests, and possibly meaning for them large displacements of labour ? I cannot think that this House will deny that, and *I say quite frankly that I cannot deny that claim.*"

We anxiously scanned these words, looking for loopholes from which the Prime Minister might escape from giving his support in future to the principle of women's suffrage; but we found none.

This speech in effect made the Liberal Party into a Suffrage Party; it therefore indicated an enormous advance in the parliamentary history of our movement.

Our future course at the time was not all quite such plain sailing as it may appear now to those who only look back upon it. The skill of the parliamentary leader consists in providing steps or ladders from which his followers can advance from a more backward to a less backward position without personal humiliation, and without calling for moral courage as great as Mr. Garvin had shown when, in the leading article already quoted, he said in so many words, " I formerly thought so-and-so, and so-and-so; I was wrong." There were, accordingly, conferences within the precincts of the House of Commons between representatives of the suffrage societies and our leading parliamentary supporters on such points as the most we could safely ask for, and the least we could be induced to accept. At these conferences Sir John Simon took a very leading part. When he was present we felt we had as our ally a man of an extraordinarily alert intelligence, capable at once of appreciating our point of view, and with unequalled readiness in showing how it could be carried out. I remember his coming in late at one of these conferences in a committee-room of the House of Commons; we had been expounding a particular point to a group of M.P.'s who seemed neither to understand its significance nor capable of offering any suggestion as to its realization. The atmosphere changed directly Sir John Simon took his seat at the table. "Yes, I see the importance of your point," he said at once; "and you can give effect to it," he added, taking the current Special Register Bill in his hand, " by an amendment in line 5, clause 2. I will speak to the Prime Minister about it this evening." It was an immense relief to our anxieties to have a man of this practical and capable type working for us. On August 22nd he handed in to the clerk at the table of the House of Commons the following resolution; it never materialized, but it indicated the line which an important group of our friends in the House were taking, and the general agreement that had been arrived at by the great majority of suffrage societies:

" That, in the opinion of the House, the Parliament to deal with industrial and social reconstruction after the war should be elected on a wide and simple franchise exercised by both men and women, and therefore legislation establishing such franchise is urgently required and should be passed during the war."

From this point onwards it is no exaggeration to say that Sir John Simon was, from a parliamentary point of view, the organizer of victory. The only real obstacle which now confronted us was the plausible plea that, however desirable women's suffrage was in itself, it was not the time during the

most gigantic war in history to raise this great
question of constitutional reform. It was our business to show that *now was the time* when such a
reform was not only desirable, but absolutely necessary. The new register and the new qualification
were needed without delay unless millions of the
best men in the country were to be disfranchised on
account of their national services. Women should
be included in the new register on the grounds given
by Mr. Asquith in the speech just quoted. When
we were attacked, as we were, by antisuffragists
for our lack of patriotism for raising our question
during the war, we had an easy answer. We had
not raised it. It had raised itself as a consequence
of the war and of the peculiar character of the qualification laid down by former Parliaments for the
occupation franchise.

It was some time, however, before the Government
itself grasped the situation from this point of view.
Before Parliament adjourned for a short vacation
in August, 1916, Mr. Walter Long, a typical English
country gentleman, then Colonial Secretary, a
Conservative and antisuffragist, made it clear that
he too had withdrawn his opposition to the enfranchisement of women. It was to him we owed the
suggestion that the whole question of the parliamentary register and the qualifications for voting should
be referred to a non-party conference, consisting of
members of both Houses of Parliament, and presided

over by the Speaker of the House of Commons.
He said, after reciting the difficulties of the situation:
" It is our duty, one and all . . . to set ourselves
to find a solution which will be a lasting settlement
of a very old and difficult problem." Mr. Asquith
concurred, and, answering by anticipation those
who argued that it was unpatriotic during the war
to be considering questions of franchise reform,
said that it was " eminently desirable " that those
not actually absorbed in the conduct of the war
should work out a general agreement as regards
these difficult questions of parliamentary reform.
The Electoral Reform Conference, with the Speaker
as chairman, was appointed in October, 1916, on
the reassembling of both Houses after the recess.
Of course it was not only women's suffrage which
it was asked to consider, but the whole franchise
question, including adult suffrage, plural voting,
proportional representation, etc. The Speaker,
Mr. J. Lowther, had a high reputation for fairness,
for great personal tact and courtesy, for humour,
and all which it stands for in the management of
men, but he was believed to be a strong antisuffragist.
The question of women was not emphasized in
Parliament when the conference was appointed, but
there can be no doubt that it was the real motive
power which had created it. The members of the
conference were of all parties and of both Houses,
and, according to the Speaker's knowledge and

belief, suffragists and antisuffragists were given an equal number of representatives on it. I always said that it was an illustration of the intense strength and vitality of our movement that, though the conference was proposed by one antisuffragist (Mr. Long), supported by another (Mr. Asquith), and presided over by a third (the Speaker), yet, as a result of its deliberations, some measure of women's enfranchisement was recommended by a large majority of its members. The conference, in fact, provided one of those ladders, referred to on a previous page, which enable men to escape gracefully from an untenable position. It held its first meeting on October 12th, 1916. Sir John Simon was a member of it, and a remarkably skilful leader on our side. He was ably supported by Mr. (now Sir) W. H. Dickinson, Mr. Aneurin Williams, Sir William Bull (Conservative), and Mr. Goldstone (Labour). The deliberations were kept absolutely secret. The N.U.W.S.S. asked to be allowed to give evidence. The request was declined. We then drew up a memorandum emphasizing the chief points on which we had desired to give evidence. A copy of this was sent to every member of the conference. A large number of resolutions from political associations, town councils, women's societies, trade unions, trade and labour councils, etc., supporting the claims of women to representation were also sent to the Speaker as chairman of the conference. The report was not published until January 28th, 1917. But the mere existence of the conference began to influence the action of Parliament much earlier than this. On November 12th, the last of the Government's Special Register Bills was withdrawn. The Bill was condemned by the House because the Speaker ruled all widening amendments out of order, and as the House desired widening amendments the Bill collapsed.

In the interval, before the conference had reported, the whirligig of time brought about another Cabinet crisis, which was eminently favourable to us. Mr. Asquith's Government fell, and in mid-December Mr. Lloyd George became Prime Minister. On Christmas Day, 1916, I received a letter from a very important public man, who told me that now was the psychological moment for taking a forward step in the direction of the immediate enfranchisement of women. He had angered me by assuming that, because we had not rioted, and had throughout the war only sought to serve our country, we had done nothing. So I told him in outline what we had done, and why we had done it. He replied: " I am going to read your letter at the Prime Minister's to-morrow." On December 27th I heard from him again. " I talked for some time last night with the Prime Minister, who is very keen on the subject [of women's suffrage], and very practical too." After this I knew our victory in the immediate future was secured, however the Speaker's conference reported.

It was at first questioned whether the Cabinet crisis and the formation of a new Government would not mean the suspension of the work of the Speaker's conference. But in answer to a specific enquiry the new Prime Minister emphatically expressed his desire that the conference should continue its labours. After three and a half months' work the report of the conference was placed in Mr. Lloyd George's hands. It unanimously recommended thirty-three very drastic reforms in the franchise, the most important of which were to base the parliamentary franchise for men on residence and not on "occupation," the adoption of proportional representation, and a great simplification of the Local Government Register. On women's suffrage the conference was not unanimous, but by a majority, which we were privately assured was considerable, it recommended that some form of women's suffrage should be conferred.* This was hailed with almost universal enthusiasm by the Press. There was a general chorus of approbation and congratulation.

* The report of the Speaker's conference was dated January 27th, 1917. The clause recommending woman suffrage ran as follows:

VIII. WOMAN SUFFRAGE.

The conference decided by a majority that some measure of woman suffrage should be conferred. A majority of the conference was also of opinion that if Parliament should

The changes in the franchise for men amounted
in effect almost to manhood suffrage; but the suffrage
for women which was recommended amounted
practically to household suffrage for women, with
a higher age limit than that fixed for men. For
purposes of the franchise women were to be reckoned
as "householders," not only when they were so in
their own right, but also when they were the wives
of householders. There was some outcry against
this on the part of ardent suffragists as being deroga-
tory to the independence of women. While understanding this objection, I did not share it; I felt, on
the contrary, that it marked an important advance
in that it recognized in a practical political form a
universally accepted and most valuable social fact—
namely, the partnership of the wife and mother
in the home. We did object to, and strongly pro-

---

decide to accept the principle, the most practical form would
be to confer the vote in the terms of the following resolution:
"Any woman on the Local Government Register
who has attained a specified age, and the wife of any
man who is on that register, if she has attained that
age, shall be entitled to be registered and to vote as a
parliamentary elector."
Various ages were discussed, of which thirty and thirty-
five received most favour. The conference further resolved that if Parliament decides to enfranchise women,
a woman of the specified age who is a graduate of any
University having parliamentary representation shall be
entitled to vote as a University elector.

tested against, the absurdly high age limit for women (thirty to thirty-five) suggested by the Speaker's conference, especially on the ground that a very large proportion of the women working industrially would be thereby disfranchised. It is only fair, however, to mention the motive which had prompted this recommendation. One main objection of the antisuffragists to our enfranchisement was that the number of women in this country was about one and a half million in excess of the number of men. It was therefore plausible, although fallacious, to say that women's suffrage would result in making over the government of the country to women. What was desired by the friends of women's suffrage in the Speaker's conference was accordingly the creation of a constituency in which women, though substantially represented, would not be in a majority. The changes in the representation of men would, it was believed, raise the number of men on the register from eight to ten millions; while the number of women enfranchised, as householders and wives of householders, would not, as it was thought, be more than six or seven millions. This, it was correctly anticipated, the House of Commons would accept with practical unanimity, whilst the fate of a wider franchise would be, to say the least, doubtful. The thirty years age limit for women was quite indefensible logically; but it was practically convenient in getting rid of a bogie whose unreality a few years' experience would probably prove by demonstration. We remembered Disraeli's dictum, " England is not governed by logic, but by Parliament."

A similar but more objectionable method of reducing mechanically the number of women voters had been adopted in Norway in 1907, and had lasted for six years, after which women were placed on the register on terms exactly the same as those for men. Events in the Session of 1919 show that it is very unlikely that the higher age limit for women will be maintained in Great Britain for so long a time. It may here be mentioned that the actual numbers both of men and women enfranchised by the Reform Act of 1918 turned out to be larger than had been calculated when the Bill was before Parliament. On the first register compiled in 1918 there were over 7,000,000 women, and the official figures of the number of men and women on the revised register published in 1919 were: men electors, 12,913,160; women, 8,479,156.

From the date of the presentation of the report of the Speaker's conference our parliamentary success went forward rapidly, smoothly, and without check. On March 29th the Prime Minister received a great deputation of women war workers, organized by the N.U.W.S.S., representing every possible form of active service by which women had worked for their country during the war. The deputation

also had the support of between thirty and forty
women's organizations, including nearly all the existing suffrage societies, besides such well-known bodies
as the British Women's Temperance Association, the
National Union of Women Workers, the National
Organization of Girls' Clubs, and the Women's
Co-operative Guild, etc. It had been the intention
of this deputation to ask the Prime Minister to
introduce without delay legislation based on the
recommendations of the Speaker's conference. But
we found ourselves in the joyful position of being
a day after the fair; for on the previous evening in
the House of Commons Mr. Asquith had moved
a resolution calling for the early introduction of a
Bill on these lines. The whole debate which followed
had dealt, not exclusively, but very nearly so, with
the question of the enfranchisement of women.
Mr. Asquith had again emphasized his conversion,
had compared himself with Stesichorus, who had
been smitten with blindness for insulting Helen of
Troy, adding, " Some of my friends may think that,
like him, my eyes, which for years in this matter
have been clouded by fallacies and sealed by illusions,
at last have been opened to the truth." In the
debate which followed every leader of every party,
Conservative, Liberal, Labour, and Irish Nationalist,
supported the enfranchisement of women, thus fore-
shadowing the Agreed Bill for which the N.U.W.S.S
had asked in the previous May. Mr. Lloyd George,

the new Prime Minister, took an important part in the debate, speaking with all his accustomed vigour and fervour on our side. The opposition was almost non-existent, and Mr. Asquith's motion was agreed to by 341 votes to 62. The practical unanimity of the House was reflected by a similar unanimity in the Press (the three *Posts*, however, see p. 79, still holding the antisuffrage fort). The general tone was well expressed in the *Daily Telegraph*, which said:

" The conference decided by a majority in favour of the principle of women's suffrage. The work of women during the war, the new position to which they are called in the whole industrial life of the country, are considerations which have effected a sweeping change in general opinion on this great matter; and it is by this time fairly plain that a measure of women's suffrage must be included in any reform legislation which is seriously meant."

It will therefore be easily understood that our deputation was of a very cheerful and congratulatory character on both sides. We were, however, able to make clear certain points on which doubts had been expressed. We explained that the support of the suffrage societies was dependent on our enfranchisement being made an integral part of the Bill from the first; we were determined not to sanction its being introduced by amendment. Mr. Lloyd George told us he had already instructed the parliamentary draughtsman to draw the Bill

on the lines we wished.   He also explained that the
Bill was not to be a Government Bill, but a House
of Commons Bill; it would be introduced and guided
throughout its passage in the House by a member
of the Government, and would be pushed through
by Government machinery, but Members would be
free to vote as they pleased in both Houses on the
women's clauses.   We spoke against the high age
limit for women, and said if the Government found it
possible to modify this, or otherwise to improve upon
the recommendations of the Speaker's conference
in a democratic direction, we should be gratified;
but, at the same time, our chief concern was for the
safety of the whole scheme.   We emphasized this,
showing how greatly we preferred an imperfect Bill
which could pass to the most perfect measure in
the world which could not.   The Prime Minister
smilingly signified his assent to these views.   We
desired only to press for such improvements as were
consistent with the safety of the whole Bill.

As the debates went on, and the House of Commons
majority for women's suffrage became more and more
overwhelming—the Second Reading being carried
by 329 votes to 40, and the majorities in Committee
on Clause IV., the women's clause, 385 to 55, or 7
to 1, with a majority within each party into which
the House was divided; and, again, on the last
trial of strength, 214 to 17—we felt the ground was
sufficiently solid beneath our feet to attempt an

improvement in the Bill. We therefore urged the Government to apply to women local government electors the same principle which had already been adopted by the House in regard to the parliamentary vote—namely, to admit to the register not only those women who were qualified in their own right, but also the wives of men similarly qualified. The great importance of this reform had been urged upon us by a member of our Executive Committee, now President of the N.U.S.E.C., Miss Eleanor Rathbone, herself a member of the City Council of Liverpool, and possessing very great experience of local government matters. The Labour Party gave the proposal its hearty support. But at first it was resisted by Sir George Cave, who had charge of the Reform Bill in the House of Commons. A joint deputation of women's societies and the Labour Party was organized on November 14th, but still Sir George Cave held out no hope that the Government would accept the amendment. There were vigorous protests in the House against this attitude; and our societies and other bodies bombarded the leader of the House and the Minister in charge of the Bill with letters and telegrams, urging the Government to accept for local government the principle they had already adopted for the parliamentary register. This had an excellent effect, and gave us a foretaste of the advantages of possessing, though at that time only in prospect, real political power. On November 20th the Government withdrew its opposition, and the amendment we had urged unsuccessfully on November 14th was agreed to without a division. The Report Stage of the Bill was concluded on December 7th, and the Third Reading was taken the same evening without a division.

The next stage of our battle had to be fought in the House of Lords, where we had far more formidable opponents than in the House of Commons. Lord Curzon, the leader of the House and chief representative of the Government, was also President of the National Society for Opposing Woman Suffrage. He was an eloquent and polished speaker, not beloved, but certainly powerful. We had tried to get a personal interview with him, but without success. His intended line in regard to the women's clause in the Reform Bill was absolutely unknown to us. He remained a member of the Government; perhaps, we reflected, it was to save his face and prevent his resignation that, as Mr. Lloyd George had told us, the Reform Bill was not a Government but a House of Commons Bill. Then there was Lord Bryce, from some points of view an even more formidable opponent, with all his prestige as an historian and a successful diplomatist. Lord Balfour of Burleigh was another redoubtable antagonist. We were told no man in the Upper House had more influence upon the predominant party in it. Then there was a group of well-known peers, representing both political parties, who were certain to oppose any sort of enfranchisement of women— Lord Loreburn, Lord Finlay, Lord Halsbury (these three were Lord Chancellors or ex-Lord Chancellors), Lord Weardale, Lord Lansdowne, and Lord Chaplin But we had powerful friends, too, among whom should be mentioned the two Archbishops, the Bishop of London, Lord Selborne, Lord Lytton, Lord Burnham, Lord Milner, Lord Grey, Lord Haldane, and Lord Courtney The Second Reading of the Bill went through without a division in the House of Lords on December 17th, but not without very hostile speeches from Lord Bryce and the aged Lord Halsbury, who carried his ninety-three years very vigorously. On comparing the two groups, our friends and our opponents, in the House of Lords we were cheered to see that our friends carried away the palm for youth. In so aged an assembly as the House of Lords this was a distinct advantage: very few peers are young enough to run the risk of rashness. The real fight in the Lords began when committee stage was reached, on January 8th, 1918. As a preliminary step the antisuffragists moved the elimination from the Bill of all clauses which had not been unanimously recommended by the Speaker's conference. This was aimed at Clause IV., which enfranchised women, but was opposed by the Government and withdrawn. Then came the more

direct attack, the deletion of the parliamentary
franchise from Clause IV.   This gave rise to a full-
dress debate, lasting three days.   On the second
of these—January 10th—we received, and looked
upon it as a good omen, the joyful news of the passage
through the American House of Representatives of
the Federal Amendment on Women's Suffrage with
the necessary two-thirds majority.   The House of
Lords was crowded, and excitement and expecta-
tion were very keen on both sides.   On the suffrage
side the speech of Lord Selborne was particularly
memorable, first-rate in manner, matter, and
method.   It produced a deep impression.   In the
small space allotted to ladies other than peeresses
on the floor of the House suffragists and antisuffragists were penned up together, and every shaft from
either side told with profound effect.   Before we were
conducted to our seats in the House of Lords, Mrs.
Humphry Ward had asked me, in the event of the
suffrage clause being carried, if I would support her
in trying to get it submitted to a referendum.   Of
course my reply was in the negative.   I told her
that, so far as my experience went, the referendum
was one of those instruments of government which
was most respected where it was least known, and
that I agreed with the Prime Minister in regarding
it as an expensive method of denying justice; and I
asked her why she had not used her influence to get
the referendum considered by the Speaker's con-

ference. Having missed that opportunity, I thought there was little or no chance of raising the question at this, almost the last, stage of the Bill.

As the debate went on the suffragists became more and more confident. Our whip had been sent out signed by Lord Aberconway and Earl Grey. The first had been a suffragist from his youth up, the son of one of our oldest and stanchest friends, Mrs. Priscilla McLaren, sister of John Bright. The second was the great-grandson of the Earl Grey who had carried the first great Reform Bill in 1832.

At last Lord Curzon rose to close the debate. The story went the round in suffrage circles that when this moment was reached a group of suffrage women who were waiting for news in one of the committee rooms of the House of Lords saw the door open and a policeman's head put in. He said: "Lord Curzon is up, ladies. But 'e wont do you ladies no 'arm."

Lord Curzon opened his remarks with what may be best described as the standardized antisuffrage speech: the pattern and method were familiar to all of us. His mistrust and apprehension were as great as they had ever been, and were expressed in his usual language. Then came a slight pause, and Lord Curzon said:

"Now, my Lords, I ask you to contemplate what may happen if, over this matter, we come into collision with the House of Commons. . . . Your Lordships may vote as you please. You can cut this clause out of the Bill. You have a perfect right to do so. But if you think that by killing the clause you can also save the Bill, I believe you to be mistaken. Nothing, to my mind, is more certain . . . than that, if your Lordships cut this clause out of the Bill, as you may perhaps be going to do, the House of Commons will return the Bill to you with the clause reinserted. Will you be prepared to put it back ? Will you be content, if you eliminate the clause, with this vigorous protest you have made, and will you then be prepared to give way ? Or, if you do not give way, are you prepared to embark upon a conflict with a majority of 350 in the House of Commons, of whom nearly 150 belong to the party to which most of your Lordships also belong ?"

Lord Curzon concluded by saying that he could not vote either way upon the amendment before the House, because he could not take upon himself the responsibility of " precipitating a conflict from which your Lordships would not emerge with credit."

The effect of this speech was intensely dramatic. The antisuffragists were white with rage; the suffragists were flushed by the certainty of victory. To Lord Aberconway, who was standing at the bar quite near me, I said, " What will our majority be ?" He replied, " Quite thirty." The division which followed showed that it was rather more than double this number, for the figures were: For the clause, 134; against it, 71. Both Archbishops and the other twelve Bishops present voted for the clause. Only twelve antisuffrage peers followed

Lord Curzon's example and abstained from voting. If Lord Curzon and his twelve followers had voted against the clause, it would still have been carried by a substantial majority.

The Royal Assent was given to the Bill on February 6th, 1918.

Thus ended our parliamentary struggle, which had lasted since John Stuart Mill moved a women's suffrage amendment to the Reform Bill of 1867. The real source of our victory lay in the enormous majorities by which the suffrage clauses had been carried in the House of Commons, and to the fact that every political party into which that House was divided showed a majority for the principle of women's suffrage. People used to talk about our fifty years' struggle as fifty years in the wilderness, and offer their sympathy upon the length of time we had had to work for our cause. But there was no call for commiseration. We had had a joyful and happy time, marked by victory in some phase or other of our movement all along. We had won municipal suffrage and all local government suffrages. Municipal offices had been opened. Women had been elected to be mayors in important boroughs. The education of girls had been enormously improved; the Universities had been opened; the medical profession had admitted women to its ranks; nearly all the learned societies had followed suit. Women were no longer treated either socially or legally as if they were helpless children—" milk-white lambs, bleating for man's protection," as one of our poets had called them; a fair share of the responsibilities of capable citizenship was within their reach. To those who were heard to groan from time to time over the fifty years it took us to win household suffrage for women we could justly reply that the time we had taken to win household suffrage for women had been just two years less than the time men had taken to cover the same ground. For, taking 1832 as their starting-point with the Reform Bill of that year, it had occupied them fifty-two years before they won household suffrage for themselves, and they started with the advantage of about one million of voters already in existence, and with the further and much greater advantage of the tradition of seven hundred years of freedom and self-government. We had no such advantages; we had not one vote between us; " we could not get the vote because we had not got the franchise," as *Punch* put it, and in lieu of the tradition of centuries of freedom behind us, we had the exactly opposite tradition of unbroken subjection and subordination. The best men and women in each succeeding generation helped and encouraged our movement from the days of Mary Wollstonecraft onwards. We were winning all the time, and never had any cause for despondency.

Our movement goes on all the more surely and

rapidly now that we have what all men have found essential to freedom, the power to control the Government and by our vote help to decide by what type of men the country shall be governed.

Very little now remains to be said. The N.U.W.S.S. has changed its name and extended its objects as described in the following chapter. I am in hearty sympathy with this development, but I felt that my years entitled me in the future to a less strenuous existence. I therefore resigned my presidency of the union, and it was a matter of sincere satisfaction to me that my old friend and colleague, Miss Eleanor Rathbone, was elected as my successor

CHAPTER X

THE DIFFERENCE THE VOTE HAS MADE

" In the United States the grant of women's suffrage
has made no difference whatever . . . the mere fact that
women have a right to vote makes no difference at all."—
VISCOUNT BRYCE, in House of Lords, December 17th, 1917.

THE words quoted above come strangely from the
lips of any man who believes in the principles of free
representative government. If the vote makes no
difference, why have our race all over the world
attached such enormous importance to it ? It is
bred in our bone, and will never come out of the
flesh, that the possession of the franchise is the very
foundation-stone of political freedom. Our fifty
years' struggle for the women's vote was not actuated
by our setting any extraordinary value on the mere
power of making a mark on a voting paper once in
every three or four years. We did not, except as a
symbol of free citizenship, value it as a thing good in
itself; we valued it, not as a ribbon to stick in our
coat, but for the sake of the equal laws, the enlarged
opportunities, the improved status for women which
we knew it involved. We worked for it with ardour
and passion because it was stuff of the conscience

with us that it would benefit not women only, but the whole community; this is what we meant when we called our paper the *Common Cause.* It was the cause of men, women, and children. We believe that men cannot be truly free so long as women are held in political subjection.

We have at present—November, 1919—only a very short experience of the actual results of women's suffrage. It is less than two years since the parliamentary battle was won, and less than one year since women voted for the first time, but already the practical results of women's suffrage have surpassed our expectations. It is no exaggeration to say that those most closely in touch with work in Parliament on subjects affecting the welfare and status of women were conscious of a change in the atmosphere of the House immediately after the passing of the Reform Bill of 1918.

One instance of the working of this change will suffice to prove my point. In 1902, after twelve years of hard spade work undertaken by a group of very able and experienced women, an Act was passed to secure that those women habitually practising as midwives should receive adequate training for their calling. The case for such legislation was overwhelming. In over 70 per cent. of the births in this country the mothers were attended by midwives. The death percentage was unnecessarily high, especially from puerperal fever.

Remedial legislation on such a matter called forth no party passions; so the case for the training of midwives was extremely simple and free from complication. But a certain amount of opposition was manifested by the least enlightened section of the medical profession; and this for a long time was the chief barrier in the way of getting any Government to adopt the Bill and use their power to pass it. As I said just now, it took twelve years to overcome this obstacle. But the Act was passed in 1902; experience proved that there were many weak places in it. No provision had been made for the payment of doctor's fees where, in difficult cases, it was desirable that the midwife should have the aid of a medical practitioner. Neither had any provision been made for the payment of travelling expenses for members of the Central Midwives Board, and other expenses incidental to the efficient carrying out of the Act. No doubt the promoters of the legislation of 1902 were well aware of these " weak places," but dared not raise a discussion on them for fear of jeopardizing the whole Bill. So matters stood until the passing of the Reform Act in February, 1918. Then, that same year, before any woman had voted, the Government produced the Midwives Amending Act, 1918. Mr. Hayes Fisher, now Lord Downham, was in charge of it in the House of Commons, and explained its object as being not only to amend the " weak places " already referred

to, but added that it also aimed at " attracting to
this great profession . . . a high class of midwives.
. . . We want them more in quantity . . . and
we want to improve them in status." No one had
ever spoken in this tone in Parliament of midwives
and their occupation before women were enfranchised. Words of this kind would probably have
wrecked the Bill of 1902, as many doctors were
extremely jealous of midwives acquiring any professional status at all. But the amending Bill went
through rapidly and quietly. The lives of women
in childbirth were taken account of by Parliament
in quite a different spirit directly women acquired
the status of citizens.

It would be easy to give other examples, and I am
tempted to add an appendix to this chapter, giving
a list of Acts of Parliament specially dealing with
the welfare and status of women passed year by year
between 1902 and 1919. There are many more
entries in the shorter period than in the longer.
This in itself indicates some of the difference which
women's suffrage has made.

As soon as might be after the Royal Assent had
been given to the Reform Bill in February, 1918,
the various suffrage societies held their several
council meetings to discuss their future action.
Some societies dissolved and formed themselves
into women cititzens' associations. But many resolved to go on working for objects closely allied

with their original purpose. The N.U.W.S.S., meeting in council in March, 1918, by a practically unanimous vote resolved to extend its " objects," including in the new programme what had formerly been its sole object—" to obtain the parliamentary franchise for women on the same terms as it is or may be granted to men " ; but adding to this two more objects—namely, " to obtain all other such reforms, economic, legislative, and social, as are necessary to secure a real equality of liberties, status, and opportunities between men and women " ; and " to assist women to realize their responsibility as voters." The last of these was an indication of the sympathy of the N.U.W.S.S. with the women citizens' associations which were quickly springing into existence.

We should have acted more logically if at the same time that we enlarged our objects we had also adopted a corresponding change in our name. However, on this matter being put to the vote, the old name was retained by a large majority. Many of our members regarded our name as soldiers regard their flag or regimental badge, and were, from motives of sentiment, averse to giving it up.

However, a year's experience proved that it would be really useful and tend to prevent misunderstandings if we changed our name in accordance with the extension of our objects. Therefore, by formal vote of the council in 1919, as stated on p. 155, the N.U.W.S.S. ceased to bear its old name and became the National Union of Societies for Equal Citizenship. We hope that the letters N.U.S.E.C. will soon become as well known and be as much beloved by its members as the N.U.W.S.S.

At this same council meeting of 1919 changes were adopted in our method of attacking what had now become our principal work—viz., the achievement of a real equality of status, liberties, and opportunities between men and women. We had learned in the last twelve months that the field thus covered was so vast that success was jeopardized if we scattered our energies over the whole of it. We therefore resolved henceforth at our annual council meetings to select a limited number of subjects deemed ripe for immediate action, and to concentrate on these, so far as practical work was concerned. The first selection for the year 1919-1920 was thus indicated:

1. We demand *equal pay for equal work*. And we demand an open field for women in industrial and professional work.
2. We demand the immediate reform of the *divorce law* and the laws dealing with solicitation and prostitution. An *equal moral standard* must be established.
3. The Government is in favour of *widows pensions* in principle. By constant pressure we mean to make the House of Commons turn principle into practice. We demand *pensions for civilian widows*.

11

4. Women must speak for themselves as well
   as vote. We want to extend the *women's
   franchise*, and we are determined that
   women candidates holding our equality
   programme shall be returned to Parliament at the next election.
5. At present women are not legally recognized
   as the guardians of their children. We
   are working to secure *equal rights of
   guardianship* for both parents.
6. Lastly, we are demanding the *opening of the
   legal professions to women.* We wish
   to enable women to become *solicitors,
   barristers, and magistrates.*

The walls of our Jericho have not fallen at the
first blast of our trumpet, but we have made great
progress in promoting the principle of equal pay for
equal work, and with the familiarizing of the British
public with women as candidates for Parliament.
Since the General Election two or three women have
been candidates, and one, Lady Astor, has been returned by an immense majority.

Another important success in 1919 remains to be
chronicled. It is the inclusion in the Charter of the
League of Nations of a clause rendering women,
equally with men, eligible to all appointments in
connection with the League, including the Secre-
tariat. This clause was inserted during the Paris
negotiations after deputations of suffragists from
the Allied Nations and the U.S.A. had waited upon
all the Plenipotentiaries. They were most cordially
and sympathetically received: but the definite

success of their efforts was in the main due to the active and whole-hearted support of President Wilson, Lord Robert Cecil, and M. Venizelos.

In the passing by the Government of their Sex Disqualification Removal Act more has been done than we ventured to ask for in the sixth item on our programme—not a bad harvest for one Session, when we remember the twelve years' work necessary to get the Midwives Bill of 1902 passed into law, or the thirty-two years' hard labour before a Nurse's Registration Bill was turned into an Act.

I do not propose in this brief chronicle to enter into a detailed description of the differences between the Government Bill and the Women's Emancipation Bill introduced by the Labour Party, and carried through all its stages in the House of Commons, notwithstanding Government opposition. The Labour Party's Bill after this triumph was torpedoed in the House of Lords, and the Government Bill was pushed forward in its place, and eventually carried into law. The Bill of the Labour Party was much more comprehensive and sweeping; it did what it professed to do, and removed completely every legal inequality between men and women, including placing women on the parliamentary register on the same terms as men. This was probably the reason why the Government objected to its passing into law, and got it defeated in the House of Lords.

For, according to all precedent, a large extension of
the electorate should be followed as soon as possible
by a General Election; and it is not very wonderful
that the Government did not desire this under present
circumstances, and while the new Parliament had
been less than a year in existence.   In some respects
the Government Bill goes beyond No. 6 in the
demands of the N.U.S.E.C.   It opens to women,
whether married or unmarried, the duty, within
certain limits, of sitting on juries and acting as
magistrates.   It makes it clear to the Universities
of Oxford and Cambridge that they have the
power, when they choose to use it, of admitting
women to membership.   It opens the legal profession to women.   But its most disappointing
provision relates to the entry of women in the
Civil Service.   It opens the Civil Service to them,
but with certain restrictions.   It does not proceed
on the lines of the Government promise of November,
1918, " *to remove all existing inequalities in the law
between men and women.*"   The Government reserve
for themselves the right in this matter to proceed
by Orders in Council.   It is true the Solicitor-
General said in the House on October 28th, 1919,
that he wanted to " have the power to differentiate
somewhat in favour of women in order to give them
a better and more equal opportunity than they have
at the present time."   We are frankly suspicious of
these offers of something better than equality.

Equality before the law is a hundred times more stable guarantee for justice than favouritism. Women over and over again have said they are not out for privilege, but for equality of opportunity. Major Hills, who was in charge of the amendments to the Bill promoted by the women's societies, said with brutal frankness that the meaning of the clauses promoted by the Government was "that all the higher-paid posts in the Civil Service will continue to be reserved to men." These Orders in Council will have to be closely scrutinized.

Nevertheless, when we remember that between 1902 and 1914 only two really important Acts bearing specially upon the welfare and status of women had been passed—namely, the Midwives Act, 1902, and the group of Acts, dating from 1907 to 1914, dealing with the qualification of women as candidates in local elections—and that since the passing of the Reform Act of 1918 at least seven important measures effecting large improvements in the status of women have rapidly gone through all their stages in both Houses of Parliament, we shall not be slow to appreciate the fact that the women's vote has made a very big difference indeed. The Act which rendered women eligible for Parliament, introduced in the Commons late in the autumn Session of 1918, went through both Houses in about a fortnight. In the Lords it was adopted without opposition.

Not of great importance in itself, but significant in its implications, was the quiet removal of the heavy grille of the Ladies' Gallery of the House of Commons in the summer of 1918, and the opening to women on equal terms of the Strangers' Gallery. Part of the grille has been preserved for the London Museum, and part will be kept in the House itself. It may be hoped that it will be put up in some appropriate place, with waxen dummies behind it revelling in the Oriental seclusion which recommended it to the Commons for about seventy years. One great discomfort of the grille was that the interstices of the heavy brass work were not large enough to allow the victims who sat behind it to focus it so that both eyes looked through the same hole. It was like using a gigantic pair of spectacles which did not fit, and made the Ladies' Gallery a grand place for getting headaches.

Suffragists are not labouring under the impression that because women now have votes no further reform is needed in our representative system. A large proportion of suffragists are probably in favour of proportional representation, and would favour its adoption mainly on the ground that it would secure a much fairer reflection of the whole nation than the present system, which may, and frequently does, result in the practical exclusion from representation of large masses of the voters. A good deal of education and spade work in spreading the principles of proportional representation are necessary on this and other important reforms, but now that women form a very considerable portion of the electorate they have at least the satisfaction of knowing that their views on this and other important political issues count for something, and are actually studied and considered, so that things work out much more rapidly than ever before in the direction they desire.

The enfranchisement of women, especially the immense addition to the women municipal electors, has put the position of women in local elections on quite a new footing.   Formerly, when there were only about a million women voters on the municipal registers of the three kingdoms, and these, in considerable numbers, were either aged or on the brink of old age, they were a negligible quantity.   They were neither admitted to the men's organizations nor consulted by them; the candidature of women for locally elected councils was cold-shouldered or opposed by all the party organizations; but the situation is quite different now.   The women local electors have increased from one million to eight and a half millions, and, besides this, women are also parliamentary electors; the result is that all the parties encourage the candidature of women, and are pleased to have one or more women's names on their own tickets.   Thus the number of women elected in the recent borough council elections in London bounded up on November 1st, 1919, to nearly two hundred. Chelsea, which never returned a woman before, now returns ten; Westminster returns seven; Marylebone returns four, and so on; and the results in many of the country towns were equally remarkable. (See the *Common Cause*, November 7th, 1919.)

Some time ago, in one of my controversies with Mrs. Humphry Ward, she lamented the very small number of women offering themselves as candidates in local government elections. I pointed out that the qualification for candidature was such as to exclude, in a large degree, the mass of the younger and more vigorous women; also, that the small number of women holding the local government franchise, coupled with the fact that they had no parliamentary vote, rendered them negligible from the party point of view, and I suggested to Mrs. Ward that the best way of increasing the number and improving the status of women concerned in local government would be to secure the abolition of their political disabilities. Events since February, 1918, have more than justified my argument.

Besides the positive gains to women and to the whole country which women's suffrage has brought about, it is satisfactory to note that none of the disasters so freely prophesied by the antisuffragists have materialized. The prophets themselves seem to recognize that they were the baseless fabric of a vision now utterly vanished even from remembrance.

APPENDIX

A LIST OF ACTS OF PARLIAMENT SPECIALLY
AFFECTING THE WELFARE, STATUS,
OR LIBERTIES OF WOMEN PASSED IN THE UNITED
KINGDOM BETWEEN 1902 AND 1919
(BOTH INCLUSIVE).

1902. *The Midwives Act.*—This Act aimed at securing for women in childbirth attended by midwives a reasonable security that these should have received a proper training. The Act was in many ways imperfect, but, such as it was, it took twelve years' hard and absorbing work from a group of able women to get it passed.

1905. *Married Women's Property Amendment Act.*— This Act rendered a married woman capable of disposing of a trust estate without her husband, as if she were a *femme sole.*

1907. *Qualification of Women (County and Borough Councils) Act.*—A similar Act was passed for Scotland in the same year, and for Ireland, with modifications, in 1911. These Acts removed the disqualification of sex and marriage, and rendered eligible on local councils married women living with their husbands, and daughters living with their parents. Fourteen years' strenuous work up to 1907 was necessary to secure their adoption. The necessary legislation was announced in the King's Speech as part of the Government programme of that year. It was the first time in the 700 years of British parliamentary history that an extension of the civil liberties of women had occupied such a position.

1914. *County and Borough Councils Qualification Act*, and similar Act for Scotland in the same year. These Acts provide for men and women alike a residential as distinct from the rate-paying qualification.

1914. *Affiliation Orders Act* sought to improve the position of the unmarried mother, but was very imperfect on account of its failure to provide any proper machinery for carrying it out.

1918. *The Representation of the People Act* (passed in February, 1918).—It placed nearly eight and a half million women upon the registers of voters in parliamentary elections. It also multiplied the number of women local government electors from one million to over eight and a half millions. It applies equally to every part of the United Kingdom.

1918. *Eligibility of Women Act* (November, 1918) rendered the election of women to the House of Commons a possibility. No work was required to get the Act passed. It was all but unopposed. Owing to the very short time between the passing of the Act and the General Election the opportunity for women to select constituencies and work up their candidature was very inadequate. Nevertheless, there were seventeen women candidates, one of whom, in Ireland, was elected.

1918. *Affiliation Orders (Increase of Maximum Payment) Act*, 1918, amends the Bastardy Laws

Act of 1872, which fixed five shillings a week as the maximum which the father could be made to pay towards the maintenance of an illegitimate child, raising this sum to ten shillings a week

1918. *Midwives Amending Act*, 1918, removes some of the weaknesses of the Act of 1902, and is sufficiently described in the foregoing chapter.

1919. *Sex Disqualification Removal Act.*—This Government Act has already been sufficiently described. The wider and more sweeping measure introduced by the Labour Party passed all its stages in the House of Commons, notwithstanding Government opposition.

1919. *The Intestate Moveable Succession (Scotland) Act* enlarges a Scottish mother's rights of succession to the intestate moveable estate of her children.

1919. *Nurses' Registration Act*, 1919.—Trained nurses without the vote had been working for registration for thirty-two years. The principle of registration was accepted by the Government, and the Act embodying it carried into law the year following the enfranchisement of women.

1919. *The Industrial Courts Act* was improved by the Government accepting the amendment of the Labour Party that one or more members of these courts should be women.

It will be seen from the foregoing survey of the legislative activity of Parliament in the eighteen years under review that they divide themselves into two unequal portions, 1902–1914 and 1918–1919. The war years are omitted for obvious reasons. In the first and longer period of fifteen years we find five measures of varying importance—that is, at the rate of one to every three years. By far the most important of these measures are the Midwives Act, 1902, and the series of Acts dealing with the qualifications of women for local government elections; both of these were due to years of hard work— twelve in one case, and fourteen in the other—of very active and efficient women's societies. In the second, and far shorter, period, of less than two years—February, 1918, to November, 1919—we find seven Acts of value and importance slipping through Parliament without any trouble at all; ministerial swords leaping from their scabbards to remove impediments from the path of the free citizenship of women. This is the " difference " the vote has made.

INDEX

BILLING AND SONS, LTD., PRINTERS, GUILDFORD, ENGLAND